It's a Long Way to Tooting Broadway

Reginald Cambridge

Copyright © Reginald Cambridge 2015

The right of Reginald Cambridge to be identified as the author of this work has been asserted by him in accordance with the Copyright Designs and Patent Act, 1988.

A CIP catalogue record for this title is available from the British Library.

eBook ISBN 978 1 943730 39 1
Paperback ISBN 978 1 514 66457 5

Typeset in Garamond 12.5 pt.

"It is so important that my generation and the generation beyond continue to read such memoirs of determination and sacrifice of 70 Years ago".

Michael Woodhouse

CONTENTS

	Foreword	ix
	Prologue	xi
1	The Military Beckons	1
2	Barrack Life	9
3	The Army From Behind Bars	15
4	Soldiers To Farmers	27
5	Tunisia, Where The Heck's Tunisia	33
	Maps: North African Campaign	51
6	Sicily, An Island Respite	55
	Maps: Sicilian Campaign	61
7	Italy & The Battle Patrol	63
	Maps: Italian Campaign	83
8	Bombing Of Monte Cassino	89
9	Sailor Uncle Bill & Monkey	95
10	Fourth Cassino Battle	101
11	The Commandos & Back To Blighty	113
	Photos: World War II	127
12	Civvy Street, Not Paved With Gold	133
13	Poacher Turned Gamekeeper	139

14	Marriage & The Intelligence Corps	147
	Photos: My Family	157
15	355 Field Security	163
16	Once Again A Civilian	173
17	Back In Uniform	179
	Photos: My First Two Malayan Postings	191
18	Holland & Germany Postings	199
19	Malaya, Hong Kong & End Of Service	209
	Photos: Hong Kong Posting	217
	Photos: The Children	221
	Photos: Reunited After 60 Years	223
	Acknowledgements	227
	Appendix I: Rest In Peace	229
	Appendix II: Dennis Lionel Scaife	231
	Appendix III: Lt. Col. John Woodhouse MBE MC	233
	Appendix IV: Eric Gordon Monsey	235
	Appendix V: Reflections	237
	Appendix VI: Malaysian Medal	239

FOREWORD

At the insistence of younger family members I've tried to give a recollection of my life, of memories that will remain with me until I die. I have done nothing special, just journeyed through life trying not to make too many mistakes.

I may be getting on a bit and not as physically fit as I once was but my memory is sound although dates and names may have faded.

One thing I do promise is that every incident in this, I suppose, autobiography, is based on true events. Finally, by its very nature, a write up of my life is probably of more interest to the writer than anybody else. Yet I hope my family and perhaps others may derive some pleasure in reading this account of my life.

Reg Cambridge

PROLOGUE

We were milling about at the drill hall when the bombs started dropping. It was June 1940. The raid was one of several we had recently. As the bombers moved away word came through houses in Western Road had been hit. An NCO of the volunteers appeared. "We may be able to help," he said. A Humber car or something of the sort stood at the kerb. The owner shouted "Get in". There was a rush for the car. I was beaten to the seats. The driver lowered the window. "Stand on the running board and hang on," he said. He took a passenger on each side. With my arm with the LDV band hooked around a window upright we shot off. Down to the Broadway, left at the Underground. Past the public baths, over the railway bridge of Blackshore Road and onto Colliers Wood Underground where we turned left past Fry's Die-castings. Here the road divided, Church Road to the right, Western Road ahead on the left.

Two houses had been hit. The walls of one virtually gone. The first floor hanging at a crazy angle. Smoke and dust still clouding the bricks and broken mortar. Domestic goods mixed with smashed masonry. Several figures lying prone with helpers around them. An ambulance drew up and medics took over. In truth there was little the group of LDV could do to help.

On the other side of the road groups of householders stood silently watching. At one gate a mother with her hands protectively resting on the shoulders of two young girls, presumably her daughters. My attention was taken by the older of the two. I judged her to be about fourteen years old. What was particularly noticeable was the beautiful auburn hair falling to her shoulders. To this sixteen year old she made quite an impression. I turned back to give the men a hand. I wasn't to know this young girl was to go through the agony of losing her father to cancer in the next two years. I wasn't to know she was to be my friend, lover and companion for the major years of my life. But as the sirens sounded the all clear, I remembered her and I was to find I also had been noticed, by a young girl with steady grey eyes and auburn hair falling to her shoulders.

CHAPTER 1
THE MILITARY BECKONS

The bus stopped at Mellison Road, just by Barnes the piano store. A five minute walk and I would be home and have to start explaining. Not looking forward to it.

Across the road, up past the Tooting Public Library and into Eswyn Road. At 98, I hooked my fingers through the letter box to pull out the door key. My mother was in the back garden feeding Donald Duck. The only duck I ever knew that couldn't swim. Mum stood silently looking at me, a piece of bread between her fingers.

It had been a week since I had spoken to her. Living in an air raid shelter doesn't cost me anything but I did need to eat now and again. She'd given me some small change that day. I'd skipped out before my father came home and we had another row. "I've got something to tell you Mum," then blurted "I've joined the army". There was a bit of a silence, I saw her lip quiver. Then "Well you'd better come in then."

That day, of October 1940, in a sense brought us together again. For four weeks I had been living in various air raid shelters but mostly under Hemmings the bakers. I had walked out of my job and declared I'd had enough of work. This caused my father to indicate that no work meant his eldest son had better wake up to reality and stop being a pain-in-the-arse. That was how I'd finished up sleeping in dirty, dark, air raid shelters. When Dad came home, on hearing my news a truce was formed and I was back with my family.

I'd been thinking of joining up for a while and had discussed it with my mate Tommy Clayton. "Think I'll wait till I get called up," he said.

I could see myself flying a fighter plane, zooming around the heavens. Seeking a recruiting office was surprisingly difficult. It seemed that the nearest was a good bus ride out to Nonsuch Hill near Ewell. There I found three recruiting offices, Army, Navy and Air Force.

The RAF turned out to be a big disappointment. Asking my age the officer in blue suggested consideration if I came back in six months and maybe he could do something for me. Or perhaps a job on the ground would suit me. Standing outside once again, I felt deflated. The romance of flying had flown out of the window. Six months to wait. Bloody war would be over by then!

Moodily I considered my options. With the RAF out of the picture I thought about the Navy. Sea sickness, torpedoes and the fear of water…! I marched into the unknown and the Army Recruiting Office.

It was here I found a friendly face. (I should have read Little Red Riding Hood more closely). He sat behind a bare six foot table with a large smile and a fatherly disposition. "And what can I do for you, Sir?" he smiled. Tongue-tied I said I wanted to join the Army. "Well you've come to the right place". He pulled out a sheet of paper. "Name?" I told him. "Address?" he continued, same thing, "Date of Birth?", "Twelfth July Nineteen Twenty Three" I answered. He looked up from his writing, tapped his teeth with his pencil, and slowly closed one eye. "So, Born Twelfth of March Nineteen Twenty Two. That makes you eighteen, right?" Now I understood the wink. I nodded and he wrote in my re-birth date. That was the beginning of the whole procedure. Then came the medical check. Height, Weight – 9 stone 12 pounds. Cough. Passed.

Moved on to the next room with half a dozen other volunteers where we swore allegiance to king and country with right hand raised. I was then a soldier. It was as the captain was talking about the king's shilling and the free travel ticket we were about to get, when it dawned on me that I was to be shipped to somewhere unknown and my parents were unaware of the fact!

So up went my hand as the officer finished talking. "What is it?" He fixed me with a glare. I stuttered a bit but got it out. "Can I go home first? My Mum and Dad don't know I'm joining the army!" The Captain stiffened. "Joining the Army, Sir"! He bawled at me. The rest of the ex-civilians all looked at me, grinning, "Err, Yes Sir" I said uncertainly.

The officer, a heavily built grey haired smartly uniformed man, possibly brought in from retirement, stared at me and then his face softened. Turning to a junior rank, he said "Fix this soldier up with a forty eight hour pass with his travel docs."

And that's how I went on leave the day I joined the army!

When I went through the doors of the recruiting office I knew virtually nothing of the armed forces. My father had been in the First World War – I was to discover later he had served in the Shropshire Light Infantry – he had survived this conflict but for the rest of his life he limped, the result of shrapnel in his leg. His older brother Jim, a regular Sergeant in the Hampshire Regiment, had been killed in the Dardanelles. I also know my Uncle Will had a metal plate in his head and a hundred percent war pension from his visit to France and my Uncle Gus had a permanent problem with his lungs caused by an enemy gas attack in the same country. But strangely it was years later when I was researching the family I was to find this information. I don't ever recall my father speak of the war, which ended five years before I was born.

The recruiting sergeant had spoken of putting me into

the Warwickshire Regiment and said there I would learn a trade. Hearing it would be some sort of engineering position, I said my last job had been in precision engineering and I didn't want any more of it! Looking at my address he said what I should join was my local regiment, the East Surrey Regiment. I had joined the L.D.V. Local Defence Volunteers (Lads, Dads and Veterans also Look, Duck and Vanish) some months earlier and had heard talk of Surrey units. That decided me and so I signed into the regiment.

That forty eight hour pass proved to be a blessing. All arguments between us evaporated. We were again a close and loving family. Of the three sons, no daughters, I was actually the second to be leaving home. For Dennis my youngest brother some six years my junior had been evacuated and was with a family of small holders living in Selsey, Sussex. My other brother, Eric, three years younger than me was living at home and attending a local school at Selincourt Road.

It was now time to leave. With tight hugs from Mum and advice "to keep your head down" from my father, a small brown paper parcel under my arm and some farewell money in my pocket I took off for the unknown. Feeling grown-up yet very vulnerable, I was to report to Chatham Barracks in Kent where I was to join the 70th Bn the East Surrey Regiment.

At Chatham I asked directions from the railway porter and finally arrived at a big imposing building, iron gates fronted by an armed sentry. At my approach a military policeman came to the gate and thrust his arm through for my papers. "Joining the East Surrey Regiment" I said. I was about to meet up with the first cock-up of many to come. Shoving the papers back to me the R.P. said "East Surreys left here weeks ago. You're in the wrong place, mate." I was baffled. I looked up from my useless instructions and asked, "So where are they?" "Search me," he replied. Then "Wait here, I'll try and find out. Give me your papers." With that he disappeared into a side building evidently the guard-room, whilst I stood bewildered with my brown packet under my arm, a few yards from the armed guard standing in front of his box, seemingly unaware of my existence.

Ten minutes passed then back came the smartly clad R.P. "the Battalion you are looking for is now at Milton Barracks, Gravesend," he stated. Then, "hang on, they are making out a rail warrant for you." Another half an hour and the R.P again came to the gate, with the warrant. "Good Luck," he said.

I finally arrived at Gravesend. With the sandwiches in the brown packet eaten, I was able to stow the other contents in my pocket. From the railway station I trudged across town until suddenly the barracks appeared. Walking up to the gate with the ancient cobblestones beneath my feet, I felt a mixture of apprehension and relief.

With identification confirmed a lance-corporal was detailed to take me to a barrack room in "D" Coy after visiting a store where I drew a palliasse and three rough brown blankets.

The barrack room was empty with bare bed frames against the walls. "You sleep here tonight," said the R.P. "Tomorrow you will be shown where to pick your kit up and given a proper bed space in your platoon." With that he was gone.

Next day what turned out to be the platoon Cpl of 15 Platoon, Cpl Nelson got me kitted up then gave me a conducted tour of the barracks. I said to him as we approached the building I was to live in, "So what are the blokes like?" "Well," he replied "they are a tough bunch. I reckon half of them have been to Borstal and the other half have joined up to avoid it." I was to find out there was a lot of truth in that remark.

As I settled into the platoon of some thirty trainees I got to know army life and the characters of many of my colleagues. The mainstay of the unit was the platoon Sgt. Sgt "Skipper" Cook was a real life old soldier with many years service in India and other of the Raj postings in peace and war and evidenced this fact with a chest full of medals. In the evenings to come, listening to his stories of punkah wallahs shaving him in bed, polishing and cleaning his equipment and other servant like services of past life conjured up memories of reading Kipling.

In the first few days wearing unfamiliar rough khaki newly issued uniforms that were a dead give-away of your lowly army status as a brand new trainee, we were met with condescending indifference by others. I remember standing in the dinner queue with a couple of other new lads when one asked the guy in front how long he'd been in. "Six months" said the guy." We stood silently digesting this statement. With just a few days behind us it sounded like very respectful service and we were impressed.

Time passed and gradually all awkwardness went as we carried out our training. My time with the LDV and the Home Guard meant that I knew many of the basics, so much so that I became a section leader.

A problem I began to face was the theft of bits of clothing and equipment from off my bed. I came unexpectedly into the barrack room one day. A couple of guys were about to walk off with my great coat and had been caught red-handed. One was a little guy named Watts and the other was George "Punch drunk" Avery. Both had joined the platoon around the same time as I.

Neither of them seemed at all fazed by being caught nicking. "You can put that back," I said angrily to Watts who was holding the greatcoat. Unperturbed, he grinned and said "And what if I don't?" "Then I'll knock your ruddy head off!" I said. Avery moved towards Watts and taking the coat from him said "I wouldn't do that if I were you," as he threw it back onto my bed.

I was really angry and thinking of other kit I'd had to pay to replace said "I'm going to knock your head off anyway," and sizing up threw out a punch. Some moments later, glazed eyes opening, I found myself lying on the floor. Avery was helping me up to a sitting position and I rubbed a sore jaw. It turned out that Norman "Bottles" Watts was a former ABA Champion at his weight and that George Avery was also a boxer.

That was my first introduction to a couple of rascals who were to become great mates. Norman who stood 5 ft and a half inch in his socks turned out to be great company and both had a total disregard for the rules and regulations of army life. They were the first of a bunch of fellows I got in with, which was to lead me quite voluntarily into all sorts of trouble!

CHAPTER 2
BARRACK LIFE

So time passed and finally basic training was over. The daily routine of square-bashing, parades, kit cleaning and the like continued but now we spent more time on the range firing weapons. I became a good shot. This stood me in good stead later as I won tins of 50 cigarettes during competitions.

There were some interesting characters in the platoon. Pte. Pipe for instance. A big boned curly headed Irishman with a weather beaten skin despite his young age. Entering the ablutions one day I found Pipe having his daily wash and shave. With his back towards me I noticed a two inch thick violent looking scar, the edges puckered as if stitched. An angry line it stretched from the lower right hand side of his back towards his left shoulder. Staring at the dark red weal, I said, "Jesus, Pipe, what happened to you?"

He splashed water on his face and talking into the mirror said, "My old man did that. When I was a kid. Pulled an iron wheeled cart with gear in it across my back?" Rubbing vigorously at his face with a towel, he continued. "A really nasty bastard. Most travellers hated his guts but because he was a violent and very aggressive bugger they kept away from him." Pipe was combing his hair, looking at me through the glass. "Forget now what I done to start him off that day. Anyway he's dead now." Pipe stared at his reflection. "He was found one night with his head smashed in. the police came but never got nowhere. Nobody knew anyfing, they said. Me and my bruvvers were brought up by an auntie. He might have been my ol' man but nobody was shedding any tears over him."

Pte. Kimber was a member of the platoon I got to know quite well. One day we were together in the butts, pasting patches over the targets, when he said, "I've had enough of this army lark. I'll be pissing off home soon and I won't be coming back." Sure enough his bed was found empty a few days later and he was marked down as A.W.O.L. Some months later, whilst on a spot of leave, I was in Earlsfield going to meet a girl I'd been seeing, (I remember her name was Sally Du Maurier, as I recall the same name as the cigarettes. The fags were rather classy – and so was Sally….) when along came a trotting horse and cart. With a big grin there was Kipper holding the reins. "Hi Reg, how's army life these days?" We chatted and I said "How come the Redcaps haven't picked you up?" He laughed and said there was always somebody to tip him off or give them wrong information. I knew Kipper was a hard case and lived further down in a pretty rough road in Bendon Valley. In fact as a school kid I'd had experiences of how rough and tough that particular road was. But that's another story. Every now and again I would see Kipper, always on a horse and cart cheerfully trotting around Earlsfield.

Another bunch of hard cases were the "Four Aces", as they liked to call themselves. They were a pretty unpleasant lot and were real "tea leaves" (thieves).

There were a number of ways one could get in and out of the barracks illegally. One way out was through circular windows built high in the walls of what had been stables. There would be a conveniently placed dustbin outside the wall.

One night, pretty late, shadows appeared out of the darkness and a voice said, "Here, have some cigarettes and chocolate." Dumped on the bed were several packs of twenties and bars of Cadburys. The Four Aces had been out and had "done" a shop in Gravesend.

The following day there was quite a stir. The word had gone around that there was to be a search of barrack rooms. It turned out that the guys had a kit bag full of goods they had whipped. They were now faced with the problem of hiding the stuff. High above the entrance doors to the platoon quarters was a flat area. By standing on each other's shoulders one could lay the cigarette packs and bars of chocolate flat down and unseen from below.

The search party of regimental police arrived. Lockers were searched. Bedding was searched. As we stood to attention by our beds they pulled the wooden stools out and stood on them to check out the area where the goods were hidden. Not being at a high enough angle they were unable to see anything of interest. Finally they marched out to turnover another barrack room. There were a lot of cigs being sold cheaply and chocolate being munched over the next few days. Although the four miscreants were not a very pleasant bunch they were part of the platoon and nobody was going to give them away.

It was about this time that I started getting into army type trouble. Army life had been something of an eye-opener. For one thing I was not used to the swearing and foul language. Probably the worst word I have ever heard my father use was "Bloody". My mother would not allow any bad language at home and I had been brought up to know right from wrong. Although I was certainly no "Mummy's Boy" I suppose I had developed a strong sense of awareness of injustice. I had gone to a reasonably decent school, hated maths, liked English and Composition and was quite a book worm. From as far back as I can remember I had been a voracious reader. Starting with comics, penny dreadfuls and paper jacketed cowboys and Indian sagas; wherever I went I would have a book of some sort in my pocket. At one time I used to boast that I had read every book in the Tooting Public Library including such subjects as psychology and all the other "ology's"

I think it began when a bunch of guys went into town one pay night and got into a punch-up with a group from another unit. I was playing cards with three or four other fellows in the barrack room. We wore side-caps in those days and one of my platoon members who was going into town asked if he could borrow my side-cap as some dirty swine had either nicked his or hidden it being aware he was trying to go out, which was not unusual. When we went over to the NAAFI we didn't bother with head gear and so I said he could borrow it. It was a mistake.

He and his pals had too many drinks and got into a drunken fight. It appears that finally they were chased by the other outfit and during the fight and the darkness he lost my side-cap. When drinking or on other occasions off duty, a soldier often had his cap under an epaulette on his shoulder. In any case the side-cap was easily dislodged. Whatever!

The next day I was ordered to report to the company office. To go to the office would you believe I had to borrow another guy's cap! The Lieutenant didn't waste time. "This is your cap," he said pointing to a muddy side-cap on the table before him. "Your name is inside it. Explain how it came to be found on the road outside." I had a problem. Didn't want to get the other soldier into trouble and like-wise myself.

"Don't know, Sir," I said. "When I looked for it in my locker this morning it had gone." I indicated the side-cap I was wearing. "I had to borrow this one to attend here, Sir." "Must have been stolen, Sir." "I didn't go out last night, Sir!"

The young officer stared at me. "Take this, clean it up and wear it." and then "I don't know whether you are giving me a load of balls but I'll give you the benefit of doubt, this time. I don't want to see you again, Understood?" "Yes Sir." "Understood Sir!"

I collared the soldier later and he said he'd been looking to pinch one from another platoon for me, but as I have now got mine back what was I moaning on about?

At one end of the barrack room was an open fronted fireplace. During the cold weather we received an allocation of coal. So after parades were over we'd have a fire going and with the two wooden 6ft. benches placed in a 'V' formation in front of the fire members of the platoon would grab a seat and enjoy the warmth. Pushing and pulling would be the order of the day as individuals vied for seats. One particularly cold evening the seats in front of the fire were full when George Avery and Norman Watts wandered into the barrack room rubbing their hands and enquired who would give up their seat and allow them to get warm. With no takers and the grinning occupants gripping firmly on to the benches the overcoated figures looked out of luck.

George Avery walked to his bed space, opened his locker and pulled out a tin of metal polish. Returning to the group enjoying the warmth, he said "So none of you f…..s will give a poor freezin' man a seat. Well share this amongst you!" With that he threw the part empty tin of 'Brasso' onto the fire where it nestled between the burning coals. For a moment, as the laughter and joshing died away there was silence. Then as the tin heated up the awareness of what was about to happen struck them. In the frantic scramble to get away from the burning coals the benches were knocked over. As the men made it to the far end of the room the heat expanded the closed tin. It went off like a hand grenade the sound vibrating through the room. Burning coals flew through the air, damping side stones of the fireplace split. As the smell of burning hit the noses of the men there was a rush to return the hot coals to the fireplace - or what was left of it.

The following day when the NCOs saw the state of the fireplace and asked what the hell had happened they were told something must have been mixed in with the coal issue for the men were just as mystified as they were...

Later the fireplace was repaired. It seemed from then on Avery could always get a seat by the fire whenever he asked.

CHAPTER 3
THE ARMY FROM BEHIND BARS

I didn't know it at the time but came the day my whole army life was about to change. Sunday evening, pouring rain, and I was back in barracks from a weekend pass. In the barrack room a bunch of guys were, as usual, playing cards.

I was about to take off my wet greatcoat when one of the players said, "Reg, do us a favour and get us some fags from the NAAFI." I pointed out gently that the rain was rather heavy. "It's pissing down," I said. "But okay." I will call this guy Davies just in case he is still breathing. "Change this postal order for me and get us 20 cigarettes." He passed me a folded postal order for two and six pence and generously said "And you can keep the change." Now at that time around about March 1941 the pack of 20 cigarettes cost two shillings and one and a half pence. (4 pence ha' penny, change, less than two pence in today's money).

So doing up my wet greatcoat once again I hurried over to the NAAFI.

Asking for 20 cigarettes by name I plonked the still folded postal order down on the counter. As the NAAFI girl went to put it in the till she looked at it, came back and said, "You haven't signed it," Putting it back on the counter she pulled a pen from her pocket. I looked at the P.O. and the empty signature block and rather than go back through the wet to the barrack block, I scribbled my signature. Back at the barrack room Davies stripped off the cellophane, given me a cigarette and soon the card school is puffing a load of smoke

Several days later I was summoned to Company Office.

The company second-in-command a Captain was seated and in the room was the C.S.M. and a nervous looking NAAFI girl. I was marched in. "Is this the soldier?" the NAAFI girl was asked. She looked at me and nodded "Thank you," said the Captain and the girl left the room. The Captain now addressed me. Pointing to the postal order on his desk he said, "This postal order is a stolen postal order and it has your signature on it. You are guilty of theft."

I was dumb-founded. It turned out it had been in a letter nicked from another soldier. "Sir," I said. "I am not a thief I was doing another soldier a favour." "Who is this soldier?" Well this was the beginning of a nightmare. I named Davies who said he hadn't taken the letter but named the guy who had, who said it had been a combined effort.

I think it was four of them that were eventually charged with stealing the postal order. I was charged with "receiving a stolen Postal Order." Despite the fact I hadn't been aware it had been nicked.

We had been told we would all be court-marshalled and because the guard room cells were already full, placed on "open arrest". I was assigned a cheerful friendly subaltern to be my defending officer. Hearing all the facts from me he indicated no problem and that I would plead not guilty at the court-martial.

Periodically we had to appear and be confirmed we were on "open arrest". During this time we carried on with our normal military duties. Naturally when I was first charged I had had a bust up with the card school gang but as time passed things cooled. It is difficult to be enemies when you are working on a daily basis together.

Time passed and although a date still hadn't been set for the court-martial it was obviously becoming imminent. Then one day those court-martial charged with theft were there, and then they were not! The whole bunch of them had "done a runner". When it was first discovered they were missing I was immediately arrested and bounced into a cell in the guard-room. When the orderly officer came on his rounds I protested that at each "open arrest" interview we had each given out word that we would not abscond. I had kept my word and yet I had been bunged into the nick. He agreed life (especially in the army) was unfair but there was nothing he could do about it.

It took several weeks before the Redcaps or whoever had rounded up the AWOLs and returned them to the camp where they were promptly put in cells. So was I!

The day of the court-martial finally arrived. I believe they tried several cases that day. As I mentioned earlier, rules and regulations were often disregarded and matters like going AWOL for long periods – often referred to as "desertion" assured a busy period for the visiting brass.

There we were spick and span, boots you could see your face in – knife sharp trouser creases and all the rest of it waiting in a side room when an agitated subaltern who was unknown to any of us came in and announced that due to the sudden posting of my previous and defending officer he had been lumbered with the job! He had done his best with the limited time at his disposal to study the case and had to recommend I should plead guilty and get a lesser sentence. The "card school" group had another defender and had agreed to plead guilty to get a shorter sentence.

Now I must digress here for the moment. During my "Open arrest" period I had of course given serious thought to the situation I was in. The possibility of declaring my under-age service had passed my mind. Although following my first counsels opinion I was pretty sure I would be found "not guilty". Yet spending time in military detention barracks sounded (a) exciting and (b) my army credentials in this bunch of soldiers would be assured. But after all I wasn't guilty of anything other than being stupidly trusting.

And now it was time. The double doors opened, prisoner and escort were marched in, halt, left turn. I faced three officers sitting at covered tables. The middle brass was probably from the advocate generals department. The "card school" group had already been in and found guilty. On my behalf my dozy looking defending officer pleaded "not guilty" as I had insisted, despite his advice. The prosecuting officer started questioning me. "Did I take this postal order to the NAAFI and buy goods, i.e. Cigarettes to the value of 2 shillings and a penny ha'penny?" "Yes Sir." "Did I sign the postal orders?" "Err yes sir." "Was it my postal order?" "Err no, Sir." A few more questions then he sat down. I knew I was done when my so called defending officer shuffled bits of paper and said I had no previous record of bad soldering, I was marched out, having been found guilty and given a 56 day detention sentence, the same punishment as the others had been given. I was not a happy bunny! I felt the court-martial was a farce and I had been conned first by the "card school" and then by the army. I felt resentful and from then on I had a chip on my shoulder that was going to take a few years to brush off.

The "card school" was quickly broken up with members being sent to various detention barracks. Fortunately none of us were sent to Aldershot the original "glasshouse'" with a pretty tough reputation, not that any of them were holiday camps!

After all this time I regret I have forgotten the names of most of the locations by which the D.B.s were referred to, except Shepton Mallet, which is in Somerset. It was a bit of a joke really when, kitted up, under escort and with an NCO in charge, I, with a couple of other guys started our particular journey. Nobody would tell us where we were going until we were in London. The NCO then let it be known our eventual destination was to be Scotland. Having never been to Scotland and knew little about it other than it was cold up there and they wore kilts and made a terrible noise with things called bagpipes we were baffled. We were all Londoners or at best from the Home Counties. We never did figure it out unless we surmised rightly that all the southern detention barracks were full!

I have to say that the journey up to Edinburgh by train (steam, of course, in those days) and on to, as we discovered, Dundee on Scotland's east coast was surprisingly pleasant. It was late May and the weather was warm. The escort certainly enjoyed it and we caused them no trouble, I didn't know the other blokes in the group as they were from other companies but we got on ok. We were, after all, in the same situation.

We were to find that the detention barracks had at one time been a home of correction for Scottish youths. A big two-storied grim looking building behind a high wall and having iron entrance gates at the end of a long curving drive, it didn't look inviting…

I will gloss over the sudden shock of arrival. The shouting and bawling at us by the hard faced incomprehensible Scottish warders hence forth referred to as "screws". Moving everywhere at the double I finally finished up in a long dormitory type room with beds lined along two walls and windows at the far end. I was directed to the only empty bed in the room. I was now the proud owner of a bed, a three-legged stool and a chamber pot. Later, when I settled in I was to find the importance of the pot. It was never to be used to pee in, but to keep our unofficial evening cocoa!

A couple of blokes descended upon me. "Had your pockets brushed yet?" enquired one. I didn't understand

and said so. "Pull out your pockets," instructed the other guy who was now standing with a sheet of toilet paper in his hand. They carefully brushed the debris out of my trouser pockets. Bits of fluff, dust and a few bits of tobacco dropped onto the toilet paper. They didn't seem to be too impressed with the result but non-the-less carefully moved away with their spoils. Later I found they scrounged used tea leaves, picked up leaves off the trees and would use anything else that they could fashion into a cigarette, using a page from a pocket bible. A mere find of a dog-end was like gold dust. No smoking was part of the punishment. The only chance these guys had of having a smoke was after lights out when the Screws had retired for the night. In the darkness these two would patiently sit trying to cause a spark to drop on a homemade tinder-box by striking a steel object – usually a large needle- across the base of a china mug, or piece of flint.

   I was asked what I was in for. The enquiry meant how long my sentence was. "56 days," I said. "Bloody Hell", the bloke scoffed. "You're only in to read the paper." Transpired he was doing a six month sentence. I also discovered I was the youngest in the room. I got particularly friendly with the chap in the next bed, a big built squaddie from one of the county regiments. Joe, a slow speaking man was about twenty years old.

   He filled me in about what "screws" to look out for, how to diddle extra cocoa and the advantage of having your flies unbuttoned and belt unclipped when nature called or as often happened, didn't. I'll explain later.

   Everywhere we went we doubled. Mark time, we doubled on the spot. We wore our equipment with a backpack all scrubbed gleaming white, gleaming polished boots. At all times we exercised with thick Scottish voices bawling in our ears.

We queued up for meals at the double,. Every day the meal was the same. In the bottom part of a metal container we had a type of meat and potato stew. Into this watery concoction you usually threw your lumpy rice which was in the top half of the container and was classified as dessert or afters. You threw your "Burma road" (rice) into the stew because you had a limited time to eat it.

There were a number of dormitories. Each dormitory acted like a large platoon. When the screws unlocked the doors (I think my dormitory was number 13!) and bawled out the number we clattered down the stone stairway onto the parade square and the day began. Double, double always at the double.

Each day the squads formed up and amid the usual screaming, shouting and bawling, doubled on the spot awaiting their turn to use the row of toilets. As one squad dashed back onto the parade ground doing up the buckles of their equipment, so another bunch of inmates, a screw standing there with a watch in his hand, were shouted to "go".

Theoretically from the moment the screw shouted "go" you had two minutes to evacuate your bowels. You ran, loosening your clothing as you ran into the latrines. Squatting, you did your business, wiped your arse, pulled up your trousers, did up your flies, buckled your equipment and doubled back on parade! Two Minutes! Most of the time, particularly in the beginning, you didn't want to crap. Nature wasn't calling. You had to train yourself, for it was the only chance you got during exercise hours. Inevitably the lines of lavatories were not the cleanest in the world by the time the 3rd or 4th dormitory was called forward! All part of the punishment, I suppose. Yet it was a tougher regime for a dozen or so soldiers. These were the "hard cases" who'd been sentenced before. Known as "two-timers" they had to carry FSMO (full service marching order) into the large packs of which, it was alleged, the screws would place a house brick for luck (extra weight).

Parades would finish around four o'clock and after the evening meal, each man would be issued with a certain number of used gas mask containers. We had to cut off all metal parts of these bags. The quicker you did it the more time you had to deal with your equipment. The knives were blunt and the webbing was tough making for sore hands and fingers.

Each morning the screw would march in with a wooden tray. The tray was perforated and in each hole was a safety razor. He would start at the first bed and proceed round the room chucking a razor on each bed. Without stopping, when the tray was empty, he continued around the room collecting the razors. By putting them into the same apertures he ensured the same person got the same razor each day. This was tough on the squaddies with a heavy beard. The blades weren't changed all that often. There were no mirrors in the room. Joe had quite a thick beard so it was fortunate that I shaved once in a blue moon. This was down to the fact that whenever I got "bum fluff" on my chin as a boy of fifteen or sixteen I would pull out the hairs with tweezers. For my favourite Uncle Gus, who had a heavy five o'clock shadow advised me as a kid not to start shaving too early because "shaving encouraged growth."

I would go through the motions of lathering up with the rest of the dormitory but I would have no blade in the razor! These I passed over to Joe. Turned out I was to be very thankful I had made a pal of Joe as, a few days later, while getting undressed ready for bed one night I became of interest to a frustrated "gay". At least I assume he was a homo, I was suddenly attacked by those groping hands and let out a yell. As I twisted and turned this guy was pulled off me and was given a punch and a kick from Joe. Thanks to this slow speaking man I was never attacked again.

Needless to say our accommodation was kept spotless. Every window frame, door surround and bed frame was checked for dust by an incomprehensible Scot. The floor was buffed to a permanent shine.

Each evening at lock down two large iron buckets were brought into the room and placed one at each end. These were to be used to urinate in, throughout the night. As I mentioned earlier no one ever thought of peeing in his own piss pot, which was solely for cocoa. The screw in charge of our room was a hulking great bear of a man with a booming Glaswegian accent.

One of the problems with the iron buckets was that each morning they were probably an inch or so from the top and needed to be handled with care, as they were taken down to the latrines to be emptied and cleaned ready for the following night. Now there is no accounting for the actions of nature and it was used for more than just peeing, in the hours of darkness.

One day in came this Glaswegian, I'll call him Jock – and seeing the yellow liquid just an inch off the edge of the buckets he blew a gasket. Bawling a stream of what was probably a selection of Scottish invective we were given to understand that (a) he was angry, and (b) if it happened again he'd kick the whole lot over.

Well the inmates tried their best but still needed to pee, fart and the desperate to go one step further. The following morning in came Jock. He marched up, chest out, stick under his arm to the nearest bucket which was not too far from my bed.

There he stood eyes bulging. He glared at the immobile liquid which was just about level with the edge. "Aye warned ye, ye dirty bastards did aye nay warn ye!" With that he put his size twelve boot against the container and gave it a violent shove.

The piss shot out spreading in a large circle soaking our pristine polished floor. Shit stood like islands in a yellow sea. We stood mouth open, unbelieving. We never thought he would do it.

Jock swivelled, stuck out a finger the size of a banana and pointing it at me and the soldier next to me, boomed "Clear this up." To which I replied "with what?" "Ye have bloody hands," he said "use them!"

We held our breath, tried not to throw up and handled the turds back into the bucket. The smell was to say the least, unpleasant. Under the Scots' direction we poured half the contents of the other bucket into the emptied one and very carefully carried them out of the room down the concrete stairs to the latrines.

It took days to clean the stained floor and the smell lingered longer. Strangely the buckets managed to keep within measurable depths after that incident yet none of us could understand how, because nature still kept calling.

So the days passed. One got into a routine, for each action could be anticipated. All fears of the immediate future dissolved. Sunday mornings and church parade were looked forward to, not because of being particularly religious or wanting to confess our sins. Sunday was a rest day in that other than the parade for church no other physical action was required of us. But the most important thing was the minister. Although a Scot, we understood his soft accent. He was possibly from the borders. After each sermon he would give a brief resume of happenings beyond the gates of our accommodation. He was a kindly man.

Church service was divided into two groups. Roman Catholics was one and as I recall everybody else in another, generally, essentially C of E.

Picking up our three-legged stools we would march to our building within the walls and enjoy the few hours of relaxation. It was on one of these occasions that we heard from the pulpit of the entry into the war of Russia as our ally.

All things come to an end. I knew my sentence ended on the thirteenth of July, 1941 this would be a Sunday. No discharges took place on Sundays, but one day earlier.

Saturday was a beautiful day. Waiting at the office for our travel documents and confirmation of discharge even the Scottish screws were almost human. Three or four of us were bound for London where we would split up to return to our units. Finally, with the gateman saying "Good Luck", and "don't come back" we were out.

Dressed in field service marching order, we marched down the long drive. At the bend I turned to look at the vast iron gates. I was free, on my way back to England and it was my eighteenth birthday. 18 years old. I had been a soldier for nine months. The young lad with the parcel under his arm had long gone. A hard bitter cynical being had taken his place. The army held no fears and no illusions. Pte. Cambridge, F.G.C.M. (Field General Courts-Martial) had been reborn!

The journey to our units proved uneventful. Other than when a delightful Scottish lady entered our compartment on the journey to Edinburgh. Seeing our give-away white scrubbed equipment she guessed correctly where we had been. From a large shopping basket she brought out a beautiful Dundee cake and presented it to us. We hadn't eaten anything so tasty for ages. She explained she was on her way to see her daughter and the cake was one of several gifts. When we demurred she said she thought our need was greater than her daughter's. She was a lovely smiling lady. My opinion of those from north of the border went up considerably that day. Whoever said the Scots are mean!!

CHAPTER 4
SOLDIERS TO FARMERS

My return to the battalion coincided with a move to a new location. It was to be the first of many changes. This one as I recall was to Minster on the Isle of Sheppey. Over the next year or so we moved from location to location. Some were more pleasant than others. Great Bookham in Surrey. Ford, in Sussex, Bridge in Kent and several others. Each move was to another part of the Home Counties. This was to be of great advantage to me and many of my compatriots. The army routine was such that provided one was not listed for guard-duty or some other such task, Sunday after church parades was free of commitments. This did not mean you were entitled to be away from camp unless you had a pass for the weekend of which a few were allocated at a time. Off Duty, this often meant that with a bit of skulduggery and providing one was not on "jankers" one was able to slip out of camp and, hitch-hiking, spend a few hours at home, sometimes returning in the very early hours of Monday morning, and sometimes, if one was prepared to suffer the consequences, returning after a few days "absent without leave" (AWOL).

I have to admit a large part of my service at this time was spent doing something of the above, or indeed paying for my "crimes". The guard room in each location became quite familiar to me. There was a downside, as I recall. My 'holiday' in Scotland (during which my pay was stopped) and the light fingers of others in the company resulting in payments for replacing equipment caused my weekly pay being reduced to a few coppers. I believe I am right in saying I was actually paid sixpence a week from which a deduction of four pence was made for "barrack damages".

This was something of an army racket to pay for such things as broken windows (which, if broken, were never repaired!).

I remember when being stationed at Ford Aerodrome where the platoon was quartered in empty houses, of putting one penny each Friday evening on the bare mantel piece over the empty fireplace. This was for cups of tea come Saturday morning when the NAAFI van visited. Can't recall what I spent the other penny on when I went into town. Living on the poverty line caused much thinking of how to increase our finances. There were several of us in similar plight.

One wheeze was to go out into the surrounding fields and tracking the rabbit runs we'd place traps for the rabbits. We'd maybe catch two or three rabbits a week which we sold to the local butchers for sixpence each. This, plus a few other things caused a cordial dislike of the presence of the armed forces by the farming community which was reciprocated.

In between exercises and other military duties we became unpaid farm labourers. The front line members of the armed forces are not known as the P.B.I. (poor bloody infantry) for nothing. It seemed that whenever a multi-person job required labour we were 'volunteered'. A farmer wanted his potatoes pulled, or Brussels sprouts collected or cabbages cut. We would, in groups be marched out to the fields in fatigues and be instructed in the wondrous arts of rural labouring. With hindsight looking back at those years, is to understand the necessity and urgency of procuring food for the population. Shortages of everything abounded, including labour. Farmers had many problems, but to young London born lads who, lets face it, generally regarded those from the countryside as swede bashers or plough jockeys or carrot crunchers albeit in a cheerful and friendly way it was not what they had signed up for. Actually the main cause of friction between the disgruntled soldiery and the farmers was really down to two things. Firstly, the high handedness of their officers to whom they were just morons who did what they were told and the apparent surliness of their rural bosses. Of course working cutting, bending, handling and loading in often freezing and wet weather didn't help. Perhaps the final straw or considered insult was the strong rumour that remuneration for our labour was respectable sums paid to the officer's mess. Whatever it was, it was sufficient reason for us on one cold, miserable day, when we were being criticised for slow production, for a bunch of us to down tools and tell the red faced farmer to get stuffed.

Needless to say action was swift. The half dozen objectors were marched back to their lines charged and confined to barracks, which only made our resentment worse. I decided some R & R (rest and relaxation) was called for and promptly went AWOL, once again.

Now at this time I was seeing a girl who lived in Kennington, a tram ride from where my family lived near Tooting Broadway. Scrounging some money from my parents I would catch a tram up to the Cut in Kennington and spend time with Betty Crichton and her family. Betty was a lovely girl, we got on very well together, which I suppose was fortunate as her muscular elder brother was locally respected as a successful boxer!

Now, I believe the trams stopped running at midnight but one every hour throughout the night would make its noisy clattering journey to Tooting. I'd left Betty later than usual one evening after midnight. Having just missed a tram and knowing I would have to wait an hour for the next one, I decided to walk. Somewhere between Clapham

North and Clapham Common I spotted a café, still open. Fancying a cup of tea I crossed the road and pushed open the door. I was dressed as always, in battle dress. The café appeared to be completely empty other than the fat unshaven proprietor behind the counter. It was a typically scruffy place smelling of fried food and stale tobacco. But it was stuffily warm. Ordering a cup of tea I suddenly heard a burst of female laughter then a trapdoor on the proprietor's side of the counter was slowly raised and out climbed a smiling woman in her early twenties. The grinning café owner turning to me said jokingly, "Looking for business?"

The woman, seeing me standing there, said "Hello soldier." Then, "You's looking lonely, come and join us", glancing towards the trapdoor. It was then I caught on. "Sorry Love", I replied. "Short of cash, I'm afraid." "Don't worry, soldier. We are not working at this time of night. Bring your cuppa down and have some company." Two things dawned on me. One was of course they were 'on the game' and the other was the woman's Scottish accent.

So saying it looks like we are both off duty or words to that effect and she was a long way from home I followed her down the steps to a basement room with table and chairs. Seated and welcomed me with friendly smiles, were 3 other women. The conversation was relaxed and humorous. The Scot, whose name was Sandy explained she hailed from Glasgow. She had been 'down south' long enough for her Glaswegian dialect to have eased up and become generally understandable. We had an animated discussion on the merits of Dundee when I mentioned my visit to her homeland, and I heard some interesting stories of their activities around Clapham Common.

When I finally left their cheerful company I realised I had missed another tram. So I continued my journey marvelling at the ways and occupations of some people and their generosity.

Another occasion when I was in the Kennington area my luck was to run out. Strolling down Newington Butts one day, minding my own business, I heard two motor bikes slowing down behind me. Glancing back I realised I was of interest to a couple of Redcaps on motor bikes. There didn't seem to be a lot of point in running. "Let me see your pass, soldier," said one. Ah, well. I'd had a week or so of freedom so I acknowledged with good grace I was AWOL. Seeing I wasn't about to cause them any problems they weren't as obnoxious as usual. Indicating I was to pillion ride on one bike I settled behind one of the cops and we rode off with the other riding escort, to their Whitehall headquarters. Checked in, I was locked in cell number three, which I had got to know quite well by now, to await a posse from my unit, probably from the regimental police. The food wasn't bad and anyway I wouldn't have to pay for the journey back to barracks. At least, not with cash!

CHAPTER 5
TUNISIA, WHERE THE HECK'S TUNISIA

I had been hospitalised with a skin infection and had been instructed on discharge to report to a Hull transit camp for a reposting. My time with 70th Bn East Surreys was at an end. I quickly realised, as I prepared to go overseas things were getting serious, for I was about to be rebadged. I was to remove my East Surrey cap badge and replace it with an East Kent one. Now, it may seem rather stupid, bearing in mind all the trials and tribulations I had experienced in the "Mutton Curries", as Londoners referred to the East Surreys, but I felt rather affronted.

Now the Royal East Kent Regiment, known universally as "The Buffs" was a fine regiment with a long history, but most strangely I had a deep seated sense of loyalty to my original Regiment. I know every infantry man feels the same, but like it or not I was now a soldier of the 5th Battalion the Buffs.

All sorts of rumours flew about as to our foreign destination despite the fact there weren't too many countries in late 1942 and early 1943, where the British had a foothold.

Passing over the military preparations and the brief embarkation leave the day came when we entrained and come the darkness slid out of the Clyde in an over-loaded troop ship to join a convoy. We had correctly guessed, and as our equipment indicated, we were heading for North Africa. My memories of that journey were sea sickness, hammocks, Housey Housey, losing all my money at poker and brag then playing chess, which fortunately cost me nothing, the fear of enemy submarines and a stark awareness of the possibility there may not be a return journey.

The voyage took a while, but finally we made it safely to Algiers. A whole new world! The smells, heat, colours, white buildings and white robed Arabs. Quite exhausting, in more ways than one! For as we marched off the docks weighed down with our kit and equipment we found out our destination was a transit camp at a place named Maison Carrie, quite a few miles away. The air was full of swearing and complaining. Soldiers wouldn't be soldiers if they didn't let off steam by verbally moaning and groaning, it keeps them cheerful!

Maison Carrie the following morning. The re-enforcements all called on parade. To be addressed by a sweating Sgt-Major with his stick under his arm. "Men" he addressed the assembled infantry men from a number of regiments. "The 1st Battalion the East Surrey Regiment has suffered casualties and urgently requires re-enforcements. All East Surrey men present will therefore, on my command, take a step forward." He then, calling the men to attention, issued the command. "All Surrey men one step forward, March!"

A number of men stepped forward. I was one of them. The rest of the parade was dismissed, and the East Surrey men were instructed to report to the company office. I thought I'd better explain to the Sgt. Major the small matter of being a Royal East Kent soldier volunteering and stepping forward with the other East Surreys.

To say the warrant officer was upset was something of an understatement. His eyes bulged. I swear I saw steam coming out of his ears. He poked a sun burnt finger an inch from my nose. "You realise I may have to call everyone back on parade, you f...ing idiot." He called a

Sgt. "Put this man on a charge." He swung back to me. "Company orders tomorrow morning!" He snorted. "Get out of my sight!" Yes. I think I had upset him.

  The following morning I was standing outside the Company Commander's tent waiting to be marched in. Again the parade was being formed up. The C.S.M spoke to the Sergeant who came over to the Company Office. "You" he said, pointing to me "Join the parade."

  Hastily I lined up with the rest of them to hear the Company Sgt. Major announce the following statement "The 1st Battalion East Surrey Regiment has suffered more casualties. It is in urgent need of replacements. All those wishing to volunteer may do so, after which men will be nominated to join. Volunteers to take one step forward." So for the second time I moved out of line. The earlier charge was conveniently forgotten and I was on my way to being re-badged and becoming an East Surrey man once again.

  It snorted. It blew clouds of thick black smoke. Clanking, screeching, shaking, the engine pulling a long line of ancient coaches slowly and painfully moved out of the station. We were finally heading into Tunisia and the front line. Fears and apprehension were dissipated into stowing our equipment, commandeering hard wooden seats and excitedly leaning out the glassless windows to watch the station gradually disappear into the distance.

  This journey was to remain with me as one of the most memorable and strangely happy experiences I have encountered. For several days we travelled with a feeling of complete freedom. Stripped to the waist in the hot and sooty air, all discipline relaxed, with N.C.O.S. farther down the train and out of sight, we slowly, laboriously passed through Arab villages with running, jumping groups of smiling children hands held out for sweets thrown to them by indulgent soldiery. We would sit on the bumpers between the carriages revelling in the slight breeze on our browning bodies, waving to white robed locals as we passed isolated huts and farms. On one occasion we clanked and stuttered into a siding where water for the boilers and coal for the engine were taken on board. On the adjacent track was a stationary engine with wooden sided trucks in tow. The trucks were piled with compo boxes. We stared unbelievingly. Within seconds boxes of army rations were being transferred and shoved under wooden seats. As our train slowly, hissing, restarted its journey, we unpacked goodies of tinned food, powdered drink, corned beef and other delights. For each composite box of rations contained sufficient for 10 men including toilet paper, sweets, matches, lovely tinned puddings (my favourite was treacle sponge!) and so on.

The coaches were reminiscent of those in old cowboy films, with a wooden rear deck enclosed by a metal waist high rail. As we chuntered along, we sought to heat tins of rations. The rear deck was the obvious place to build a site for a fire where cans of tea and so on were continuously on the go. So it was no great surprise but rather annoying when burning embers and steaming cans suddenly disappeared. The fire had burned and charred the tinder dry floor boards and we were looking down through the hole at the rail track.

Sitting on the bumpers or the covered curved top of the carriage, a mug of tea in my hand, a lighted cigarette in the other, my hair blowing in the hot breeze, stripped to my shorts seemed to be the perfect way to enjoy the passing hours.

Unfortunately it was not to last. Pulling into a Tunisian station we were back in the real world. Chaotic orderliness is possibly the only way to describe our disembarking, sorting kit and joining our respective units.

There was urgency in the instructions. With the Surreys re-enforcements shepherded into transports we moved off.

Prior to our arrival 1st Surreys, with the main force of 1st Army and being part of 11th Brigade, 78th Battleaxe Division had been experiencing a more or less successful advance towards Tunis, their ultimate goal, in hard fought battles during the late period of 1942. But when almost twenty miles from Tunis a massive counter attack by the German Army led by the German Panzer Divisions pushed back the allied forces. Virtually all the salient points, towns, hills which had been a series of bitter battles by both the American and British forces were lost.

By the time the massive counter attack was held the Surreys as with the many infantry battalions had suffered heavy casualties. By the early days of December when they were finally able to re-group they had lost more than half of their original strength.

At the same time the weather deteriorated. Cold heavy rain added to the men's misery and set in for several weeks. Roads became impassable due to thick mud. But this period enabled the units to recover their wind, build up and replace lost guns and equipment and prepare to attack once again the obstacles to taking the prize of Tunis. But this could not happen until better weather in the coming spring.

It was during this period of watching and waiting I, with other re-enforcements were to join the battle experienced men of the 1st Bn resting in a reserve position, where we would be embedded in different companies.

I had had a few days to settle in my company but was still feeling something of the "new boy". Their comments, jokes and remarks of officers and NCOS were above my head. Many men were obviously very weary. Some didn't say a lot.

We were able to move around reasonably freely and it was here that I met up with the guy who was to become a lasting friend. Dennis Scaife of around my own age, who had been with the 70th Battalion albeit at a later date than myself and had also, joined the 1st Battalion with a group of re-enforcements. What we had in common was both hailing from Tooting, South West London. Dennis always seemed to have a permanent smile and enjoyed cracking awful jokes like, "Are you alright?" "Yep, all down one side." He was still cracking the same dopey jokes 60 years later, but that's another story!

We hit it off straight away and shared a slit trench where we would sit yarning about the snooker hall, or the tea-stall by the lavatories at Tooting Broadway, or the trams that turned round at Blackshaw Road to return noisily towards the heart of London. Dennis was a few inches taller than me and skinny with it. I would tell him if he stood sideways to the enemy they couldn't hit him. We were to go into many battles together.

Dug in on the forward slopes of the hill we faced the enemy across the valley unseen on the opposing hills. Nestling in the valley was a deserted farm house. On a day when the sun shone and the enemy were quiet or appeared to be, Dennis and I were sitting in a forward trench with a pair of binoculars between us with instructions to keep an eye on the valley and observe any movement of the enemy. Dennis was using the glasses when he said "there is something moving in the farmyard." He passed the bins to me, with a grin. "All I can see are chickens moving about," I said, returning the glasses.

"A couple of those would make a good meal," he mused. We looked at each other. "It's quiet, nothing happening. Could get there and back without any fuss." We thought about it. Then, "Let's do it."

We slid out of the slit trench and made our way

forward, cautiously, across the valley to the farmhouse. It had been shelled in the past. The ruined building was enclosed in hedges of prickly pear. Half a dozen clucking chickens were strutting about the dirt farmyard raising little clouds of dust as they sought something to eat. Carefully we moved in on them. That's when the fun started. You could say we were rather inexperienced in such matters. The scrawny birds would wait till we moved near them, then with a cluck, a hop and a run, they would be off. After five minutes of useless chasing the birds had all sought sanctuary in and under the dense hedges of prickly pear! It looked as if we were going to miss out on chicken soup. As we got our breath back, Dennis said, "I've had enough of chasing theses buggers" with that he raised his rifle, took aim and fired. Feathers flew everywhere. What was left of the carcase was pulled out from the hedge. In for a penny, in for a pound, I decided, and shot another one and another. With a couple of birds each it was time to go. That's when Jerry decided to take a hand. In quick succession we heard the hiss and scream of mortars. They exploded near enough to make us get a move on, as we scrambled towards our own lines, and dived into our slit-trench. The mortaring stopped, and the quietness of the day returned, until an irate officer paid us a visit. He was not at all a fan of the chicken expedition and went on to say so. Finally he replaced us with another pair of soldiers and we passed over the binoculars. We were greeted with large grins and offers to help with cooking the birds. But one or two said what a stupid stunt and I guess they were right.

The chicken soup was delicious!!!

I was to experience my first attack. We were given a quick verbal briefing by the platoon officer. I grasped a few points. During the night we would be drawn up on the start line and at first light we would advance forward across a valley and take the hill on its far side. It was hoped to have advantage of surprise in the initial attack. Before moving off to the start line we jumped up and down to check nothing rattled. Strangely I don't remember artillery fire or any softening up the enemy in the early stages. So throughout the darkness we moved silently up to the line. No smoking or talking. Instructions were whispered. We could see the beginnings of a new day in the sky as the dawn began to break. The signal to move forward was given.

On line abreast with gaps between us we moved silently towards the silhouetted rising ground across the valley, small packs on our backs, weapons held ready. Crossing hard ground we moved into a field of growing corn. A rocket fired into the air illuminated briefly the scene. Then all hell broke loose. Three German manned machine-guns simultaneously burst into firing. Red tracer bullets spaced between unseen rounds flew in our direction. The air was again brightly lit as a second light burst into whiteness.

Somebody shouted "Get Down! Get Down!" Hurling ourselves to the ground with our Lee Enfield's forward of our bodies we laid outstretched and motionless in the field of corn. We were completely helpless. The slightest movement seemed to attract the hissing, ricocheting bullets from machine guns which were firing on fixed lines enfilading most of the valley. So much for a surprise attack! Laying there, feeling the sun warming the back of my neck, the scream of a soldier when he took a hit and nobody able to get to him I got to thinking this could be my first and my last assault on the enemy. An enemy I hadn't even seen! I have no idea how long I remained prostrate in that field. An attempt by some of the boys further forward and behind rising grounds to take out one of the machine gun nests proved abortive.

Then behind me at some distance I heard the squeal of tank tracks. Then retaliation. Shells and bursts of gunfire above our heads silenced the German machine-guns and as enemy mortar bombs began dropping we were able to move forward. After a fierce battle resulting in a number of casualties we finally took the hill. We then dug in and prepared for a counter attack. I had survived my first battle! It was only later I realised how narrowly had been my 'survival'. When I was about to 'dig in' I removed my pack to find a bullet had penetrated from the top left corner and exited through the bottom right. Just a couple of inches lower and I would have been a 'goner'.

The lower slopes and the far side of the hill became our "home" for a period. The hill appeared to be isolated by another, larger valley across which the Germans had withdrawn to a range of hills. It was now evident that the hill we had taken had been a strongly held forward position with the more formidable range of hills across the valley, their main defence. Except for the occasional shell sent over to remind us and a return shell to let them know we were still around, our particular part of the front remained for a time pretty quiet.

I don't think the hill had a name. if it did it is long forgotten. A hill in a series of hills. A dawn attack on a hill and after we'd taken it, we'd dig in, rest up, and prepare to attack the next hill. Sometimes the enemy would put in a counter-attack. Sometimes- not too often- we would be dislodged and have to take the hill all over again. More casualties. More deaths.

This particular hill was more craggy than most with patches of dead ground and large misshapen rocks which had provided some cover for the attacking infantry.

It happened after we had taken the hill following stiff opposition. As we reached the summit it appeared the enemy had withdrawn. I was slightly to the left of the majority of our men. Above me a large boulder stuck out of the ground. A few feet to its right more broken rock.

At that moment most of the firing seemed to die down.

I moved to the right of the boulder and began to move around it. At the same instance a German did the same from the other side. We were almost upon each other. Simultaneously we acted. His rifle, bayonet fixed, flashed towards me. Equally I had brought up my Lee Enfield, bayonet fixed. My finger was on the trigger and as I raised my arm I fired. The bullet took him in the chest. His jaw dropped and his legs gave way. I felt the reaction of the Lee Enfield as I had fired from the side of my waist.

Fearing others of his comrades were following him I bolted back towards a patch of dead ground. Here I finished putting a new round of ammunition into the breach. As I did so blood dripped from the stock of the Lee Enfield.

It was then I realised how close the action had been. As his bayonet had come forward he had caught the inside of my right wrist. I had pressed the trigger instinctively a split second before his bayonet came towards me.

Fortunately it wasn't much more than a cut which had missed the veins. Some seventy years later the scar has faded but each time I look at it I am reminded of the good fortune I had had, and the German.

We consolidated our positions and throughout the following days we received a number of counter attacks. Bombardments of shelling, heavy mortars, machine gun fire were followed by infantry assaults on every platoon position.

Facing us were paratroopers of the Herman Goering

Division. Several assaults were then held but with casualties on both sides. The paratroopers would fall back, re-group and again attack. On the fourth and final attack paratroopers, probably reinforced by extra troops, came flooding forward following heavy advance bombardment. Our defensive machine gunners were knocked out and we could no longer hold the hill. We had to withdraw with the loss of many casualties. A hill on our right flank held by French Moroccan troops was captured by the advancing enemy. This seriously compromised the safety of Brigade Head Quarters and gun lines in support. A counter attack was quickly prepared and another of our companies with mortar support successfully regained the hill. This hill, Djebel Djaffa was finally cleared with a number of the enemy captured, later again the Moroccan troops took over.

Later a 'recce' patrol established that enemy troops had pulled back, leaving many dead from both sides. The lost ground was once again occupied by our infantry.

At some time in early February we moved over the river Medjerda where the engineers had managed to build a Bailey bridge and took over positions from an American outfit near Goubellat.

The Battalion was stretched out covering an area of some seven miles. Our company was about a mile and a half in front of the main Battalion's position, and were on an isolated hill the Americans had called 'Fort Macgregor'. This rocky position was in an isolated position on Goubellat Plain. Here fighting patrols went out by both sides resulting in a number of causalities. Whilst at this position we became the subject of heavy bombardment followed by an infantry attack by paratroopers of the Herman Goering Division which was at first beaten off. A second attack came which was much stronger and we had to move back to our rear weapon pits. Then again for a third time they came, finally over running some outlying defences.

We had to withdraw from Fort Macgregor having suffered heavy casualties. The hill was then the subject of heavy shelling by our artillery. That night a patrol was sent out to recce the area. The returning patrol reported Fort Macgregor was a ghastly sight of dead infantry- both British and German.

Later the hill, not much bigger than a football pitch, was recaptured. The History of the East Surrey Regiment records "The Fighting of 'D' Company at Fort Macgregor was as heroic as any incident in the long history of the Regiment!"

It was early dawn when we lined up once again on a start line. Another hill to be taken, another attack with the usual apprehensive foreboding, this could be the one where our remains, lifeless or mortally injured would be found whether the battle was won or lost.

We moved forward deafened by a creeping barrage from our artillery as the sky steadily brightened the slope up which we were advancing showing little cover for the slowly moving infantrymen.

As the barrage lifted towards the reverse side of the broken rugged skyline defender's machine guns and mortars opened up. Dennis and I dropped to the ground into a slight depression instinctively as mortars blasted rocks and earth into the clearing sky. "Bugger this for a game of darts", muttered Dennis pressing harder into the earth. I was about to agree with him when a violent blow caused an anguished sound of fear from my throat. Dennis turned his head sharply in my direction questioning me with his eyes. "What's up?" he said. "I've been hit." Dennis closed the gap between us. "Where?" "In the backside," I said, unwilling to put my hand behind me. Dennis took a look, then "You've got a piece of shrapnel sticking out." He stopped, poked at my right cheek and grinning, said "You lucky bugger. It's sticking out of your emergency rations and I can't see any blood." Keeping as low down as possible and with some difficulty he tore my rear pocket apart and handed me my tin of emergency rations with a piece of 2 inch jagged and still hot shrapnel sticking out.

My backside had a painful bruise but was otherwise unharmed. The emergency ration is a tin of about 4x3 inches and 1.5 inches thick containing a solid chocolate type filling which would probably break your teeth if you tried to bite it. Every infantry soldier was issued with one which fitted neatly into the back pocket of the thick khaki trousers. Relief flooded through me and I think we both became slightly light headed.

Eventually the hill was taken and the enemy withdrew.

Sometime later having crested the brow of the hill and the guns and all firing had ceased, Dennis and myself were moving down the reverse slope when we saw two Germans walking further down and heading for trees and bushes at the right hand corner of the field.

We brought up out rifles and shouted "Hande Hoch" "Hands up". The Germans turned round to face us, dropped their rifles and put up their hands. They were probably a hundred yards or so from us. It was a nice clear day and we were feeling pretty good having survived another battle. As we moved towards them Dennis said, "What are we going to do with them?" That question was immediately resolved. As one, the two Germans dropped to the ground out of sight for there was a slight rise between us. We promptly did the same for they were now armed. Although we were above them, we knew we were more exposed and expected rifle fire any minute.

Nothing happened and we realised they had the advantage of dead ground, and were able to move unseen. So it seemed like a stand-off between us. Then we saw they had moved further down the field and were approaching the corner of bushes and trees. Standing up and realising the firing distance was now too great, we watched the pair of them at the corner where they turned round and waved. Sharing no hard feelings we waved back as they disappeared out of sight.

The idea of shooting them in the back hadn't appealed to us, and so we returned to our lines, all of us to live another day.

The battle for Tunisia was a battle for vital hills as we pushed the enemy forces slowly towards Cap Bon and their eventual surrender. Tank battles on Goubelet Plain, resulted in smashed and burning armour. The high ground had now been taken and regained. Each attack followed by preparing for the next. For infantrymen particularly, it was a slog. The enemy fought its battles ferociously. Each piece of ground fought over inevitably resulting in casualties. It all became something of a blur yet some have scarred the memory. The sweetish smell of dead bodies, particularly fierce and extended battles like Longstop Hill where I was to be dug out of my caved in trench when a shell so close that the ground heaved and showered rocks and earth above me and for a moment I thought I was dead but had only blacked out.

Waiting in a dried up river bed as shelling tries to break up the enemy. Two injured men come into view. They are Canadians. One, a young officer is helping his colleague who has his arm around the officer's neck. Blood is dripping where his foot has been blown off. The officer is hatless; shrapnel has split his head open. His brain can be seen. Medics rush to help. Stretchers appear. An ambulance jeep arrives, and the two men are stretchered on. The jeep moves slowly back down the river bed. Enemy shelling and mortaring is continuous. The air is filled with dust and rock fragments and earth shaking explosions. The scream of a shell landing near by makes us hit the ground. The dust clears. The jeep has taken a direct hit. All are dead. We move forward.

Vicious battles finally gave way to surrender by the German Forces at Cap Bon which became our last battle in Tunisia. Long columns of tired and defeated grey uniformed Germans trudged into hastily erected prisoner of war sites, their war, now over.

Sometime later, rested and recuperated we marched through Tunis. Local citizens, French speaking, crowded the streets offering wine. With music playing, smiling happy faces greeted us, with pretty French girls running alongside us putting long stemmed flowers down our rifle barrels kissing willing infantry men. It certainly raised the spirits of the victorious soldiers.

When the fighting stopped the battalion moved to Hammamet on the East coast of the Cap Bon Peninsular. This was heaven. Sandy shores and warm sea welcomed us. It was at this time I almost met my maker – not for the first time. I was never a good swimmer- this was due in part to an incident in a swimming pool when I was a young lad. I became trapped under water on my first visit. A bunch of us on seeing the beautiful placid sea stripped off and charged into the water. Shouting and splashing we played like young kids on a seaside outing. It was then I realised I was out of my depth and I was getting into difficulties. Trying to keep down the swelling panic I could feel beginning to envelope me I shouted to the happy boisterous group. They assumed I was also just having fun. Real fear gripped me for I was steadily moving farther out and away from the group. But my frantic splashing had been noticed by a quieter member of the platoon who came to my aid. Relief flooded through me when my feet touched bottom. Waving away my heart felt thanks he grinned and dived back into the sea. There was little question he had saved my life for which I have been eternally grateful. I never met him again, he was killed in Italy. I have never forgotten him.

A short time later we moved to Sousse where we began re-training. It was here we had our first sight of General Montgomery.

The battalion was formed up in a three-sided square into which Montgomery was driven. Standing on the back of the jeep he surveyed the assembled soldiers and announced the 78th (Battleaxe) Division was to become part of his 8th army. Now the 78th Division had been a large part of the 1st Army. As I understood it the 1st Army had been formed for the Tunisian campaign and its members rather liked being part of it. So when Montgomery addressed each battalion of 1st Army- each forming a three-sided square - and enquired as to whether we were proud to join the famous 8th Army he was met with a resounding "No", much to the consternation of the senior officers present.

Of all the infantry forward movements in which I was engaged I have to mention an assault which in particular sticks in my memory. Not for the detailed incident that occurred so much as the bitter – the resolute defensive fighting of the enemy. It is now one of the many battle honours of the East Surrey Regiment and several other regiments. It is the battle for Longstop Hill!

About the second week in April, 11 Brigade of the 78th (Battleaxe) Division of which the 1st Battalion the

1st East Surreys was part, were engaged in heavy fighting for 3,000 ft. high ridges known as Djebel Tanngoucha and Djebel Ang both of which over looked Longstop Hill and Medjes. The number of casualties was heavy but finally the attacks were successful leaving the way open for an attack on Longstop Hill.

1 Surreys, considerably depleted in officers and men were relieved and concentrated in the same lying up area it used before the attack on Djebel Ang and prepared for the final assault on Longstop Hill – the last peak held by the enemy. Four Battalions had been chosen to carry out the attack, although no battalion could muster more than 200 men- some far less!

A night march was made to a forward assembly area. The Germans had laid a series of anti-personnel mines besides the tracks that the Battalion had to use, causing a certain amount of confusion and a number of casualties to an already depleted force. The plan, envisaged for the attack, had the 5th Buffs and the 6th Royal West Kents clearing the foot hills of Longstop Hill after which the 8th Argyll and Sutherland Highlanders and the 1st Battalion the East Surreys were to go through and attack the summit. By dawn on the 23rd April, which was a good Friday and the Surreys Regimental Ypres Day, the Buffs had made progress on the slopes and the West Kents who had been held up by mines and machine gun fire were making headway towards their objective.

At 1130 hours, in broad daylight the Argylls and Surreys were ordered to attack. It was a hard, slow battle, the enemy having the advantage of being above us and having had time to prepare their defence positions. They defended with great determination and our casualties were severe. Next to us the Argylls were also taking casualties. Their Commanding Officer was killed and his second in command a Major Anderson won the Victoria Cross for

Gallantry in leading his Battalion. The advance up the slopes of Longstop was made through intense machine gun fire and heavy mortaring. Towards evening the Argylls and Surreys now heavily depleted were in control of Longstop Hill, newly joined by the West Kents. The whole force had been commanded by the C.O of the 1st Surreys, Lt Col Wilberforce who was awarded the Distinguished Service Order for his leadership.

Unfortunately Lt Col Wilberforce was never to wear his DSO for, sitting in his truck by a cactus hedge at St Peters Corner shortly afterwards, he was talking to his Intelligence Officer when the enemy- firing what was considered to be the final round from an 88mm gun killed the Colonel outright. Captain Wadham the Intelligence officer's lost his kneecap from the same round.

In a sad quirk of fate his batman was actually stitching the DSO ribbon on to his officer jacket at the time of his demise.

We prepared for a counter attack (which never did come). I was sitting near the brow of the hill, half deaf from the shell that had virtually buried me, with my arm around Dennis, who had fought alongside me and was now shaking with the reaction. We were not only still alive but also unscathed yet surrounded by the bodies of less fortunate comrades.

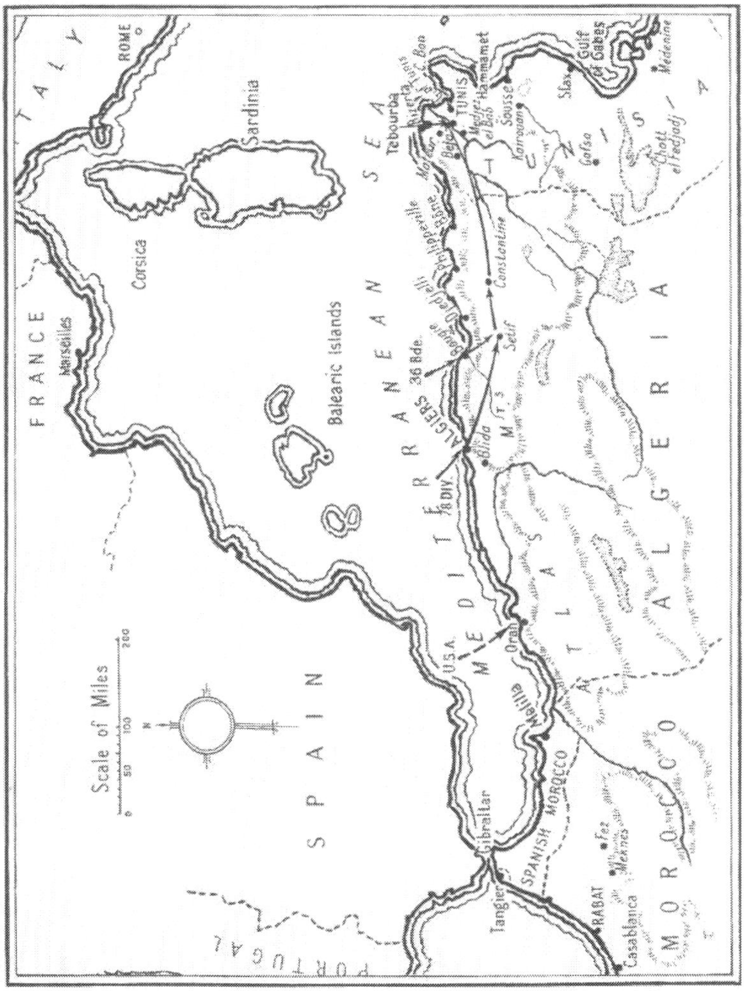

FRANCE
Marseilles
ROME
Corsica
Sardinia
Balearic Islands
MEDITERRANEAN SEA
SPAIN
PORTUGAL
Scale of Miles
0
50
100
200
Gibraltar
Tangier
SPANISH MOROCCO
RABAT
Casablanca
Fez
Meknes
MOROCCO
U.S.A.
Oran
Melilla
ALGIERS
78 DIV.
36 Bde.
Blida
Setif
Constantine
Tebourba
TUNIS
Hammamet
Sousse
Kairouan
Sfax
Gafsa
Gulf of Gabes
Medenine
ALGERIA

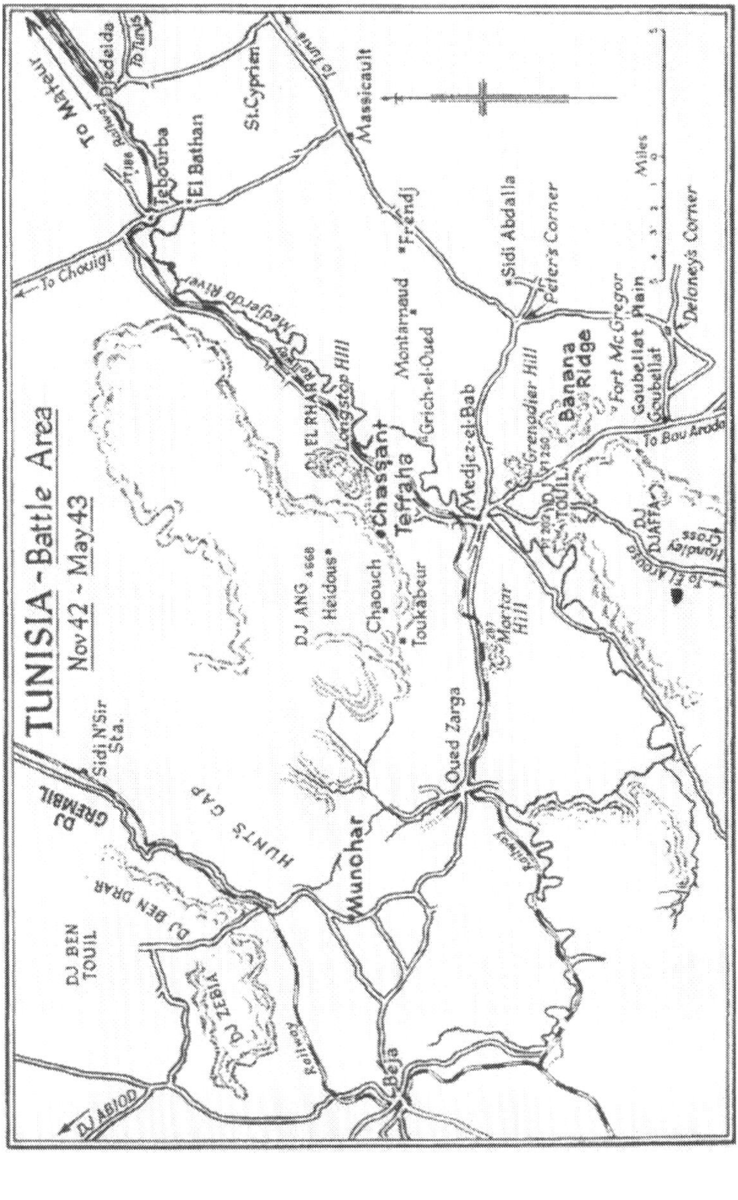
TUNISIA - Battle Area
Nov 42 - May 43
To Mateur
Djedeida
To Tunis
Tebourba
El Bathan
St.Cyprien
To Tunis
Massicault
To Chouigi
Medjerda River
Longstop Hill
DJ EL RHAR
Chassart Teffaha
Montarnaud
Frendj
Grich-el-Oued
Medjez-el-Bab
Sidi Abdalla
Peter's Corner
Grenadier Hill
Banana Ridge
Fort McGregor
Goubellat Plain
Goubellat
Delaney's Corner
Miles
To Bou Arada
DJ DJAFFA
Hendley Cross
To El Aroussa
Mortar Hill
DJ ANG
Heidous
Chaouch
Toukabeur
Oued Zarga
Sidi N'Sir Sta.
DJ GREMBIL
HUNT'S GAP
Munchar
DJ BEN DRAR
DJ BEN TOUIL
DJ ZEBIA
Railway
Beja
DJ ABIOD

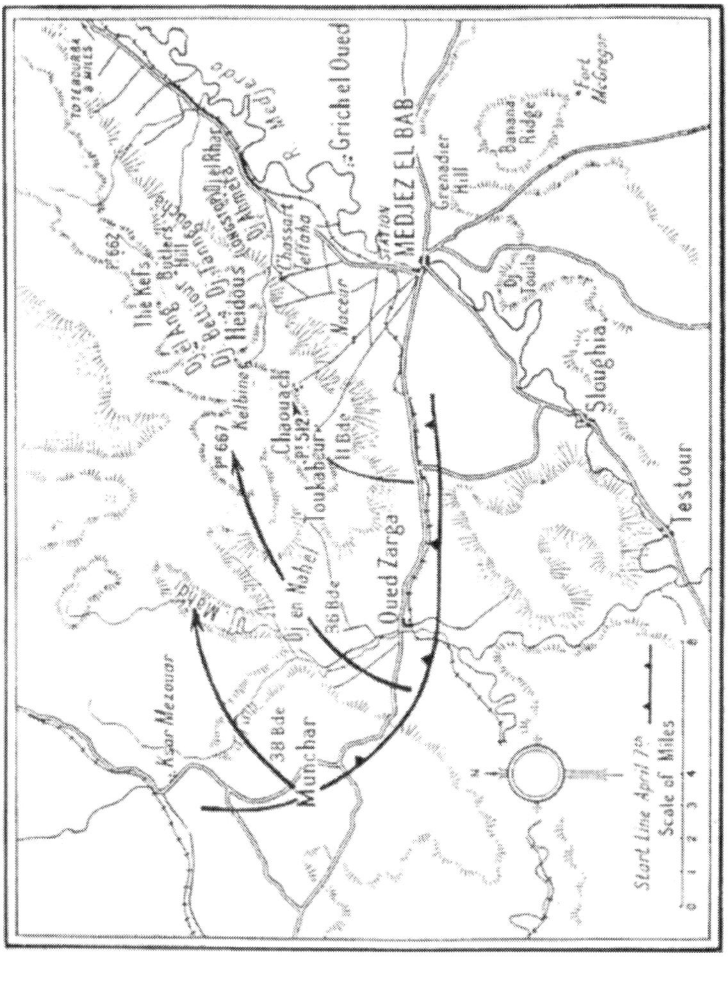
MEDJEZ EL BAB
STATION
Grich el Oued
Grenadier Hill
Banana Ridge
Fort McGregor
Sloughia
Testour
Oued Zarga
Toukabeur
Chaouach
Pt. 512
Pt. 667
Kelbine
11 Bde
36 Bde
38 Bde
Munchar
Ksar Mezouar
Dj. en Nahel
The Kefs
Pt. 662
Dj. Heidous
Start Line April 7th
Scale of Miles

CHAPTER 6
SICILY, AN ISLAND RESPITE

The invasion of Sicily took place on the 10th of July. As is the way, other ranks of the battalion knew little of what was going on but one thing for certain we could soon be joining them. Our Battalion the 1st Surreys, after a sea journey in a landing ship infantry (LSI) in which virtually every one was sea sick landed at Cassible, South of Syracuse.

By truck we moved up to Palagonia where we debussed and moved forward on foot. It was tough going. The sulphur fumes from Mount Etna mixing with the dust from the rocky ground choked us. It was hot, sticky and sweaty. Our equipment straps rubbed sores on body parts. The smell and sight of Etna was constant. Finally we rested up and then prepared for our first assault. In the dark we formed up for battle. We were to assault a hill some distance ahead. Our artillery started a barrage which was landing short. In fact was falling on our start line. Lying in the darkness with our own shells dropping amongst us scared the hell out of me and it seemed to go on for ages. There were some casualties before the barrage lifted, and we were able to move forward. Dawn was beginning to break when we arrived at the objective. The enemy became aware of our presence and opened up. Bullets flew and mortars screamed but climbing through the olive trees we took the first part of the hill. Ahead of us was a long ridge over 1500 ft high which was finally taken. From here we could see the town of Centuripe, later to be referred to often as "Cherry Ripe".

Between us and Centuripe were hills and valleys yet to be taken.

We were resting on the forward side of a hill, I remember I was talking to Dennis Scaife standing close to our young platoon officer. It was then as I looked at a bush close to the young Lieutenant I saw a hole suddenly appear in one of the leaves, followed by the crack of a rifle. I shouted to them to get under cover and did so myself. Looking forward over the short valley to the rising hillside, we saw a hatless enemy solder with bandoliers of ammunition over his shoulders waving his arm and proceeding to defiantly comb his blond hair. It was Dennis who broke the amazed silence. "I'll show the cheeky bugger," he said, and getting down behind a bren gun fired a burst at the lone figure. Whether he was on target or not we were unsure but the soldier wasn't to be seen again.

Like many towns in Sicily, Centuripe was perched on the brow of a hill. On the side of the hill were narrow terraces cut out and about 10 feet above each other. Some had olive trees on them. We found Centuripe to be strongly held and a tough place to attack. Our particular objective was the cemetery. The Germans were firing machine guns on fixed lines and having laboriously climbed the terraces to where we had a view of the cemetery any movement by us brought down heavy fire.

It was whilst sheltering from enemy fire on one of the highest terraces that we received a young soldier who had come up with a small band of re-enforcements. From our cramped position against a dirt wall we cautioned him to stay low. We returned to the business in hand firing at movement in the cemetery area. It was then I heard a cry. Turning round I saw the young lad lying with blood over his hands. He had been hit badly. A machine gun burst had caught him in the stomach. We did what we could for him but the outcome was inevitable. He died calling for his mother. He hadn't been with us for half an hour. He had told us he was eighteen.

It was a really nasty battle but eventually we overcame opposition and the enemy withdrew. The cemetery was an appalling sight. Dead of all ages were strewn everywhere. German bodies were mixed with recently buried and long buried cadavers. Body parts were everywhere. Later we were to see Italian families sadly searching and sometimes recovering their dead. We moved on. Like 'Longstop Hill' and many others 'Centuripe' was to become an East Surrey battle honour.

After a few days rest we moved down the steep slopes of Centuripe to the valley below. Crossing a river we stayed hidden in an olive grove. Adriano the next town was to be taken and our objective a hill on the edge of town. We found moving to the start line was a lot harder than anticipated. The road had been badly damaged by shellfire. It was a black night and difficult to maintain direction and contact. Artillery fire supporting the attack opened up and the noise was deafening. Explosions were getting too near for comfort and there was a strong tendency to hit the ground. With great relief we found the enemy had withdrawn. A number of dead Italians and Germans showed the artillery barrage had been effective.

Whilst resting the following night we were told to prepare to move off at first light and continue the push forward. On our right was the forbidding mass of volcanic Mount Etna. Near its base a road followed its contours. Solidified black lava was everywhere and off road made walking difficult. The town of Bronte was the next target.

Whilst moving forward the Battalion was held up by snipers and machine gun fire. It took artillery and an infantry attack before a small hill was successfully taken.

Here we rested. Gardens of fruit had survived the fighting and we were able to enjoy grapes, pears and figs. Mules were used to supply us with rations and ammunition.

Bronte was taken by another infantry Battalion and we, having passed through Bronte, were to take the town of Randazzo. Here a number of men were killed or badly injured by mines hidden in the rubble. The town had been heavily shelled. It was around this time we were met with the Germans six-barrelled weapon the Nebelwerfer, known to us as the 'Moaning Minnie'. It fired six shells rapidly with a high pitched shriek and its impact was deafening. After moving through Randazzo we rested up.

All next day American troops moved through our lines. It was to be the end of fighting in Sicily as far as 78th Division was concerned. Shortly afterwards the campaign came to an end. The Germans had fought a withdrawing action and although lost the battle for Sicily they managed to move substantial weapons, equipment and armed forces across the Messina Straits to Italy.

This was to be the next and toughest battle ground.

With the campaign over, our battalion rested and made ourselves at home in an olive grove. The general routine of an infantry man's life began to occupy our time. Kit was checked. Boots highly polished. Parades began. Rifles inspected. As life neared to normal, soldiers' attitudes became somewhat 'bolshie'. The majority of the men were after all Londoners who now had a feeling of being hard done by. Me? Well I had always had a chip on my shoulder where the army was concerned! Things came to a head one Sunday morning when it was announced there would be a kit inspection. This meant each man displaying every piece of issued kit in a particular order. There was no doubt the order was resented. Sunday was usually a day of relaxation. Many thought it unfair. As men began placing their kit in an orderly fashion I made up my mind. "Stuff that kit inspection," I said. "I'm going to have a look at this place called Sicily". As I shoved shirts and socks back into my kit bag a voice said, "And I'm coming with you". I looked round to see the grinning face of Bill Bates of the same section. My friend Dennis (Lew) Scaife declined saying he would keep an eye on my kit whilst I was gone. Bill and I tied our kit bags to an olive tree and I stuck a note above them announcing "back in two weeks".

With the sense of freedom in our nostrils we slipped out of camp. We decided to head in the general direction of the American held area and make for Palermo the capital. On the road we thumbed a lift with an American truck driver. Our general story line if questioned was to say we had been given four days leave. It turned out to be a really great period. We stayed nights with various military units of American troops. On several occasions we hitched lifts with black Americans who always on hearing our excuse for being in their particular area insisted we spent time in their particular unit. In those days black Americans were separated from white Americans. Essentially they provided support to the fighting troops. For us to sit with them to have a meal brought them some delight and they were interested in the answers we gave to questions concerning our way of life. We also stayed at times with American fighting troops. The generosity and friendliness of all is still well remembered.

It was when we thumbed a lift from a British 3-ton truck that we got a bit of a shock. "What are you doing in this part of the island?" asked the driver. We gave our usual 4 day leave patter. The driver screwed his face in puzzlement. "But your brigade is about to move to Italy," he said. At this point we had been absent for about a week. This was unexpected news. When it transpired the truck was passing near our battalion we got him to drop us off a mile or so away. Our arrival at platoon lines and our reporting to Company HQ followed its inevitable course.

We were placed in close arrest immediately and subsequently charged with Absent without Leave (AWOL). Given 10 days Field Punishment and forfeited twenty seven days pay.

With a move to Italy imminent I was told my Field Punishment would be digging toilets for an advance party to Italy. I couldn't believe my good luck! Advance parties are usually easy-going set-ups sent to prepare for the arrival of the main force. Other units had landed on the mainland of Italy before us and so sometime in September 1943 we landed at Taranto at the foot of Italy. Life seemed quite normal with the Italians friendly and inclined to help us. Mussolini was no longer a force for he had been deposed.

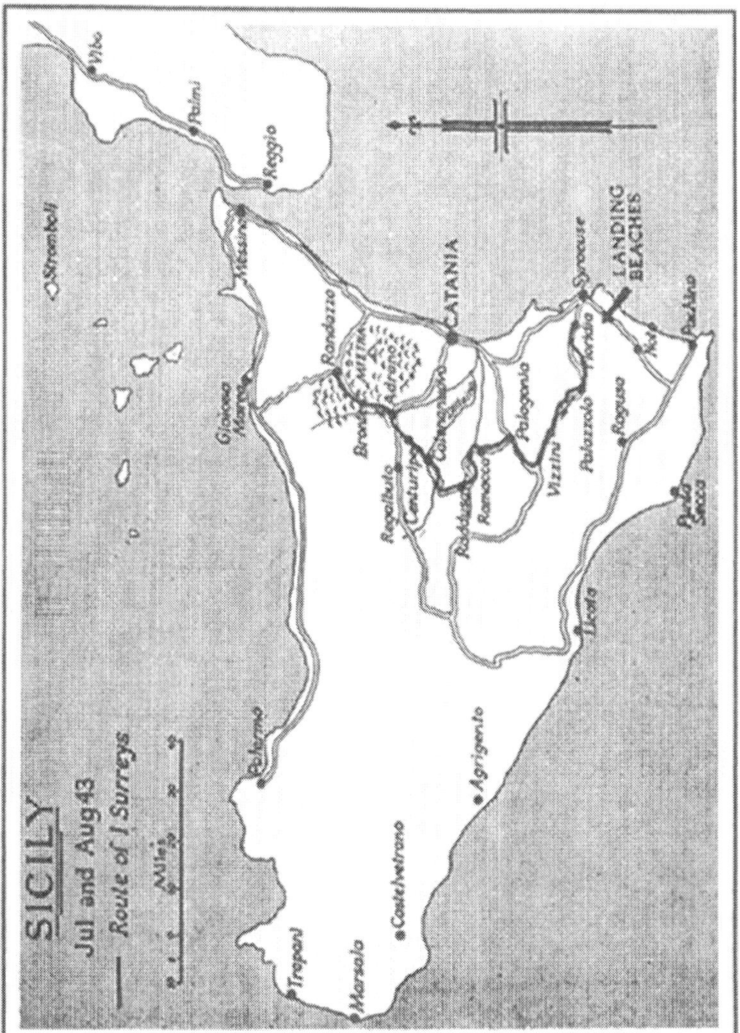
SICILY
Jul and Aug 43
Route of I Surreys
Miles
Trapani
Marsala
Castelvetrano
Palermo
Agrigento
Licata
Ragusa
Pachino
Noto
Syracuse
LANDING BEACHES
Palazzolo
Vizzini
Palagonia
Ramacca
Regalbuto
Centuripe
Bronte
Adrano
Randazzo
CATANIA
Messina
Stromboli
Reggio
Palmi
Vibo

CHAPTER 7
ITALY & THE BATTLE PATROL

With the arrival of the battalion we travelled along the east coast to Bari. Everything seemed peaceful. The first action we heard about was airborne units had taken the airfield at Foggia about fifty miles further north.

With the arrival of the trucks which had landed at Reggio we moved again up the spine of Italy. We made contact with Jerry near a place named Larino which is about fifteen miles inland from the ports of Termoli.

The attack went in to take a ridge just south of the town. The enemy brought down heavy fire of artillery and mortars. Here we were held down for several days. Finally the enemy withdrew and we were able to enter the town. The locals seemed pleased to see us. We had taken a number of dead and wounded. Larino was to be long remembered.

We stayed in this area for nearly a week probing with patrols seeking out the enemy. Our next move was to the River Trigno. The enemy were well dug in and the advance was held up. Movement in daylight was tricky as any movement brought down enemy fire. Supplies were made at night and done in heavy rain. We did little for several days, except patrolling.

Finally an assault was mounted and having crossed the river the Surreys managed to take San Salvo Railway station and the town of Capello, finally over the next few days moving up to the river Sangro. We had been told this was the first major defence position the Germans had prepared for their defence of the remainder of Italy.

Another battle over, we were resting up although

digging trenches purely as a precaution. Dennis and others decided it was my turn to make a brew so being an obliging sort of guy and having made my trench deep enough to my satisfaction I got a fire going and put on a cut-off biscuit tin of water. The rest of the section was called away to help with some duty or other. The water boiling merrily, I went to our cache of tinned food only to find our tea tin contained a seriously reduced quantity of tea. A soldier, left out of the last battle (LOB) had most likely helped himself. The remainder of the tea leaves barely coloured the boiling water. With the thirsty soldiers now on their way back and not wanting to disappoint I grabbed a large handful of reddish soil from my recent excavations and chucked it into the biscuit tin. The water changed colour. With the guys holding out their mugs and with copious doses of sugar and dried milk entered into the mixture I awaited a torrent of criticism. Blowing into the steaming mugs and with much smacking of lips they gave their considered opinion. "Lovely cup of Char!" "Been looking forward to this." I decided to keep my culinary skills to myself and said, "That's' the last of our tea 'til our next lot of rations."

The area had been moderately quiet and we had been able to get some rest. Dennis had spotted what had been a pig-sty – part ruined- as was the farm buildings and the rest of the village from previous artillery onslaughts. Strangely enough the church had partially survived. To have a roof over our heads was something of a luxury and so Dennis and I bedded down for the night despite the overpowering smell. It was only later when the weather warmed up and we were cleaning weapons, and carrying out observation of the enemy we realized our mistake. Scratching and itching we discovered we had become hosts to those biting pests lice, and it seemed, various other bugs that bite. It was not the first time we had had lice but it seemed to be excessively so on this occasion.

Jerry let us know he was still active by sending over the occasional shell. This gave one of us the idea of suggesting putting a lookout in the church tower. We found it was the intention to do so anyway, so we offered our services as voluntary observers which was happily accepted by the rest of the section who apparently were quite comfortable where they were.

Dennis and I moved carefully into the church and were able to ascend the damaged tower. Sitting back in the shadows we had a good view of the front. Checking all was quiet, we stripped to our waists. I lit the stub of a candle I'd brought with me, turned my shirt inside out, heated the handle of a metal spoon in the candle flame and ran the spoon handle along the seams of the shirt. We did the same with every bit of clothing killing most of the lice and eggs.

The following day – no longer sleeping in the sty, we did the same trick again until we were virtually free of the pests. Later we were able to move back out of the line and use the mobile bath house. Showering and replacing our clothing was pure luxury.

Here I must digress. During the period I was "holidaying" with Bill Bates in Sicily, a young officer in another company was receiving orders from his commanding officer, Lt. Col Harry Smith, to form a "Battle Patrol". The instructions had come down from 78th Division headquarters.

At this time this young officer was not known to me. Lt John Woodhouse was apparently delighted at the prospect of forming his own mini unit particularly so as the 'Patrol' personnel were to be given separate billets. He called for volunteers from the battalion's companies which he quickly received. Being 'away' from the battalion, I, of course, new nothing of this, but events were to develop. About this time elsewhere life was tough. The Salerno landing had become a touch and go situation and it seemed possible the bridge head would not be held and the British and American troops would be pushed back into the sea, such was the ferocious defence put up by the German counter offensives. In just two days it is said the American 5th Army had over 1,000 casualties.

It was around this time whilst we were resting up we heard a rumour (one of many) that a patrol of around thirty men commanded by an officer and a Sgt had been ambushed by German paratroopers on their first patrol. The officer and Sgt had escaped but the remainder had been captured without a fight! It appeared this group had been called the Battle Patrol. It appeared that several days later the Sgt had turned up, to be followed a day or so afterwards by the officer. Both were unscathed.

We, being just private soldiers knew no more than this although later heard that the officer had been exonerated from blame and the incident put down to unfortunate bad luck.

Sometime later we heard that Lt Woodhouse the young officer in question would be addressing each company in turn with the object of reforming the 'Battle Patrol'. The comments prior to the visits can be imagined. I think we may have been the third company to be addressed. Apparently at that stage there had been no volunteers…Lets face it. Infantry men tend to be a) superstitious b) cynical. Lt. J. M. Woodhouse, a slightly built figure wearing a Devon and Dorset side cap spoke briefly. Patrolling activity is not one that infantry men particularly care for, so he was not met with rapturous applause.

Dennis and I listened to him in silence. But one thing

struck me. Losing a bunch of men as he had done and then circling the Companies for volunteer replacements called for a lot of guts. If he had been rubbish the C.O would never had given him a second chance. With the speech over we returned to our lines. "I wouldn't mind giving this battle patrol thing a go." I confided in Dennis. He thought for a moment. "You join, I'll join" he said. We went over to a tent in front of which sat the young officer."

"We'd like to join your Battle Patrol" I announced. He studied us for a moment, liked what he saw, stood up and shook hands with us – not a thing officers normally do with scruffy other ranks. "Welcome aboard" he said. "You are the first to volunteer". A day or so later a soldier from another company turned up. Eric Monsey was a quiet speaking lad from Norfolk. We hit it off straight away. Some time later we were to hear the true story of the lost patrol. It had been formed with an officer, Sgt, Cpl and L/Cpl and 12 privates a total of 16 personnel.

One particular occasion for the first action by the Battle Patrol, Lt. Woodhouse had been charged with locating the enemy as contact had been broken. This part of the country is an area of low hills with farm houses dotted among olive groves. The Battle Patrol occupied a small deserted house posting a single sentry to watch for any approach along a small stream. The sentry reported a single man approaching along the stream. The officer with binoculars watched the man approach. The man was wearing a khaki drill shirt similar to ours and the Canadians who were known to be on our left flank. The soldier in khaki drill stopped and then suddenly Woodhouse saw a platoon of German soldiers running through the olive grove with the intent of getting behind us. The officer John Woodhouse instantly shouted "Run for it!" and did so himself. Unfortunately he didn't wait to see if they complied. Only the Sgt. escaped and was later separated. Woodhouse cautiously returned to the house to find it empty. There is little doubt that this catastrophe was to make Lt Woodhouse a much more cautious character and various lessons became ingrained.

Although originally few in numbers, we began carrying out patrols, mostly at night. After a time several others joined and we became a tight knit group. Carrying out Recce patrols to locate the enemy and miniature type fighting patrols we became a useful part of the battalion. We operated in groups of four. As such we were well suited with John Woodhouse, Eric Monsey, Dennis and I in turn working as Point man. Training as well as actual patrols together in actual practise made us more effective than patrols made up by rifle companies where personnel varied. The 78th Division Battle Patrol was authorised to wear the 78th Divisional badge – a yellow Battle Axe on a black background over the left breast pocket. With so few men in the Battalion so entitled we rather considered ourselves to be an elite group, particularly as we became successful in what we were about.

Although Lt Woodhouse – who became known to his personnel as "Charlie" considered his men to be rather special, another officer Capt. Toby Taylor had a different view point. "The Battle Patrol was now a permanent part of the Battalion" he said. "It consisted of all the roughs and toughs - the men who in peace time did not make particularly good soldiers, but in these conditions were invaluable". On hearing this I did wonder if Capt. Toby and I had met up at some time….

The Battle Patrol without doubt became a source of pride to its men. We would often be required to go forward and return with a prisoner. The information obtained provided knowledge of the enemy. It was during this time that an Italian, a Doctor Guido Fano formerly an officer of an Alpine unit, provided information on location of the enemy. He offered to go forward with us. As an unknown quantity the men regarded him with some suspicion. "If anything goes wrong we kill him" muttered Dennis. Fortunately everything went fine and we returned to our lines unscathed.

We continued patrolling. The weather was absolutely foul. Continuous heavy rain, bitterly cold winds made river crossings hazardous. The enemy had prepared for a long defensive action. Concrete pill boxes, barbed wire, machine gun pits and so on. There was little possibility of a successful forward advance and so patrols were continuous.

One of the patrols was particularly interesting. Guido Fano who spoke excellent English had become an interpreter for the battalion. He knew the location of a German tank arbour within the enemy lines. On the 14th of November the Battle Patrol prepared to carry out an attack on this German location, some 8 miles distant. It was a dark night when we moved off. Other than Charlie Woodhouse who preferred a German Schmeisser sub-machine gun, we each carried a Tommy gun.

Guido Fano accompanied us across the "no-mans land" part of the journey. We moved silently and carefully forward. After some miles we came to a halt. Charlie came to me and Dennis. He whispered "You two come with me." I whispered back "Where to?" His reply amazed me. "We are going to meet Guido's wife". With Guido leading we moved either side of Charlie and were guided to a single story building that stood in complete isolation. As we approached the entrance a figure appeared out of the darkness holding an ancient weapon. After muttered Italian exchanges of welcome between Guido and the cautious figure, we were ushered into the house.

Blinking in the sudden light of an oil lamp we were confronted with a large double bed. Supported by pillows was a pleasant looking woman with, as I recall, long red hair. Amazingly we were greeted by this lady in English with a Scottish accent. A Scottish lady in the middle of no-mans land in Italy! I sat dumbfounded as glasses of wine were passed around.

Returning to the resting patrol leaving Guido Fano behind, we continued into the darkness. In our initial briefing we had been informed that we would reach a deep ditch some half a mile or so prior to the enemy position.

We reached the ditch to find it was much deeper than anticipated with thick mud in the bottom. We scrambled down into the slimy base and with some difficulty made the far side. We continued until we saw the outlines of a barn-like building with armoured vehicles parked.

We had reached our objective.

Silently we spaced out and studied the layout. Suddenly a door opened in the nearby house and out came a German soldier, his rifle over his shoulder. He was silently and quickly captured and whisked away. Several of us were carrying 2 kilo explosive charges- of German origin. Some went forward towards the tracked vehicles. I moved towards the accommodation. Placing an explosive against the double doors of the house I pulled the detonator and moved quickly to the side of the house. The charge made an almighty noise in the silence as I placed and detonated a second charge under a window. The wooden shutters blew off and it began to sound like firework night as I sprayed the blown off doors and windows with Tommy gun bursts. At the same time explosives were detonated on the armoured vehicles, and what with the boys also blazing away merrily with their automatic sub-machine guns it must have sounded to the undressed and unprepared Germans like a big scale attack.

We withdrew and raced back towards the ditch, fearing the enemy would follow us. Slipping and sliding we landed in the muddy bottom. Making it to the top, we re-organised, and headed back the long journey to our own lines with the prisoner who provided valuable information. The following day the names of those who had taken part were taken, and passed to headquarters. Lt. Charlie Woodhouse was to receive the Military Cross and L/cpl Len (Timber) Woods the NCO on the patrol, the Military Medal.

The next evening several of the patrol went into town. I declined to accompany them and went to bed early. Several hours later I was roughly shaken awake. As I rubbed sleep out of my eyes I found myself surrounded by a bunch of drunks babbling on about a dead pig and did I want bacon for breakfast. It transpired in their drunken state they had chased and killed a pig. It was too big to bring back to camp. They knew in my distant past I had worked as a butcher's assistant for a brief period, which in their alcohol fuelled minds qualified me for this important task, which was, to cut off the pig's leg.

Sometime earlier during a peaceful period I had the good fortune to visit an Italian village renowned for its skillful blade making inhabitants. Here I had specified the manufacturing of two weapons. One was a stiletto type dagger and the other a longer weapon, the hilt incorporating a form of knuckle duster. Both were extremely sharp and in leather sheaths. The stiletto I wore in my belt when in action.

Removing the larger knife from my kit I followed the Vino fueled compatriots into the darkness. It seemed to be the middle of night and pitch black. They guided me into a field of growing bulbous vegetation which I quickly realised were cabbages, to the ghostly white mound.

 Shocked I stood peering through the darkness at the recumbent animal. "This is not just a pig" I said. "It's a bloody great boar!" It was massive! Enormous!

 The drunks giggled and said shut up and get cutting. Taking a deep breath I carved into a leg. Some moments later I passed to them a heavy slippery leg which they had difficulty handling in their drunken state. With the leg removed the triumphant posse staggered out of the field.

 I looked back. Silhouetted against a greying morning sky, the boar had been turned on its back. As if in mourning the drunks had tried to disguise their misdeed by covering up the carcase with cabbages. I could see the boar's stubby legs protruding towards the night sky.

 All three of them!

 I went back to bed...

 The following day there was hell to pay. The town mayor had been the owner of the boar. His favourite pig. Someone identified the culprits and a very angry lieutenant was demanding answers. I kept my head down. A compromise was made by making an apology to the Italian plus a big whip round by all the patrol members. A lot of sheepish soldiers recovering from an excess of bad wine felt the anger of the group. Secretly a few days later we served up a lovely meal of roast pork. Charlie made no comment – just enjoyed his meal.

 I reflected on the incident. If the Germans had carried it out, would the Italians have reacted similarly? When I bought the knife, from the Italian town famous for such weapons and made specifically to my instructions, I never dreamt the first and only blood on it would be from a dirty great pig.

Around this time we were given 4 days leave at Campobasso. Here are a few extracts from the diary I occasionally kept at the time.

'Proceeded on 4 days leave at Campobasso. Awful journey. Weather very cold- continuous hold ups – single line traffic. The Beaver club is very good. Saw 'He's my Guy' – Dick Foran. Started reading 'Spirit of Revolt' by Philip Gibbs'

Tuesday 4th January 1944
Saw 'I married a Witch' with Frederick March and Veronica Lake. Also ENSA Show 'Double Scotch' Buono!

Wednesday 5th January 1944
Snowed all day, might manage to stay an extra day or two. Finished 'Ask Miss Mott' by E. Phillips Oppenheim. 'Recommended in Dispatches?!'

Thursday 6th January 1944
Returned to the battalion at Campinone. Lost 400 lira at 9 card brag. Got drunk on Vino. A good time was had by all – until afterwards!

Saturday 15th January 1944
Starting off on a 4 day patrol into German line. Leave here 13:30 hrs. Here's hoping I come through OK.

Sunday 16th January 1944
Arrived Caprocotta. Aforementioned scheme off! Am going out to Atellata.

Monday 17th January 1944
Heard of atrocities by Germans to Italians. Italians make us welcome. Killed a sheep for us. Did a patrol. Nothing special.

Tuesday 18th January 1944
Another patrol. Nothing special. Getting fed up

Thursday 20th January 1944
Commence skiing

Wednesday 23 February 1944
Now on Cassino front. Patrolled- Recceing for B. Coy. Quiet

Thursday 24th February
Mr. W. and Dickinson and Owen go to river to do sniping. Surprised by 3 Jerrys – W. with his hands up. Dick fires- wounds one Jerry in shoulder and hand. Bullet goes through berretta. J's run away. All okay.

Evening: Booby trap house (P.S. Dick gets M.M). (Military Medal).

Despite the awful weather, bitter cold and ceaseless shelling from the enemy, we continued carrying out patrols across the river Sangro. The river was high due to heavy rain.

The Division had moved back into the mountains not too far from Frosalone for a short period before taking over higher ground near the mountain village around Aquaviva.

In some places the snow was 12 to 15 ft deep. Supplies

to the outlying platoons had to be pulled along on sleighs.

Time passed. Patrols continued. We moved, and moved again. The word being bandied about was 'Cassino'.

65 miles south east of Rome lies Mount Cassino. It dominates the entire area and was the only pass from south to the north. The East Surreys were spread along the banks of the river Rapido on the south side of Cassino. The entire area was in full view by the enemy observation posts on Monte Cassino. Movement could only be made at night. The Germans occupied the far bank of the Rapido. Any movement was to invite shelling from the surrounding mountain.

We carried out patrols along the banks and occasionally over the far bank of the River Rapido, trying to locate German positions and possible landing places for an assault. One of our first patrols was to the Cassino railway station. The New Zealanders had gained and then lost it a few days earlier. The Americans had tried to cross the Rapido there and failed. Rubber assault boats and other signs of the attempt were everywhere. The intention of the patrol was to capture a prisoner, but we were unsuccessful and returned to camp empty handed.

On another occasion we were trying to find where the battalions could cross the River Rapido. We were in an American rubber boat trying to get across the river. We found the river too fast flowing and taking us seaward. After some difficulty we managed to land it on our side of the river. It was a close run thing. Particularly as I have an in built fear of water and am a poor swimmer!

The weather was deteriorating. Continuous heavy rain soaked everything. The temperature steadily dropped. The rivers rose in many places to over 6 ft. deep. The rivers

Trigno and Sangro were continuously patrolled. It became an exhausting business. The Germans had based their Winter Line on the far side of the Sangro and continuously shelled the south of the river. Movement in thick mud became difficult, tiring and depressing. The Battle Patrol continued seeking possible river crossings and advanced on enemy positions.

The Winter Line, built over a period with forced labour, extended in places to 20 miles in depth. Concrete defences, machine gun posts, barbed wire, mines, booby traps, tank traps added to the defensive positions of the rivers, hills and foreboding mountains. Troops defending this line included Germans of the 65th Infantry Division and our old enemy the 16th Panzer Division.

According to an entry in the East Surreys Regimental History, General Montgomery visited our part of the front at that time and assessed the area as follows.

"What was seen was a wide river bed of many channels with a steep bank on our side, a plain on the other about a mile in width and then an escarpment with higher ground still. The approaches to the river were muddy and treacherous and the bridges blown. The river bed itself was about 400 feet across."

It was also known that the plain on the other side of the Sangro had been heavily mined with anti-tank and anti-personnel mines.

Sometime around the middle of November the Battalion moved back to Casalbordino for a weeks rest during which time we had the opportunity of visiting a mobile bath unit. This comprised of several trucks fitted with showers, and hot water. In the final truck we were able to obtain clean shirts and under clothes. It was having enjoyed these luxuries and whilst waiting for transport to return us to our unit that a staff car about to pass us, suddenly halted. From a rear window a voice called out,

"Why are you men standing there?" it was 'Monty'. I went up to the car, saluted and explained we were awaiting transport after visiting the bath unit. "What is your unit?" "1st Battalion East Surrey's", I replied. Where upon he handed me a pack of 200 cigarettes. "Your Battalion is doing an excellent service, keep it up!" said the great man. The car then sped off.

A week or so later the attack to cross the River Sangro began with an artillery strike from the 78th Division guns. The 36 Infantry Brigade of the Division attacked and established a crossing over the river and held a small bridgehead. They took heavy losses in doing so and our 11th Brigade of which the 1st East Surreys were a part, were ordered into the Bridgehead. Here the Battalion spent a week in heavy rain immediately below German defensive positions on higher ground. The incessant rain pouring into the Sangro resulted in such flooding our lines of supply were cut off until they were able to organise 'DUKWs' by the mouth of the Sangro and then by troops to the Battalion position.

Patrols by day and by night were continuous and mines caused casualties. The Battle Patrol went out often. It was on one of these night patrols that we got into a fire fight with a German Recce patrol. I was point man at the time, that is slightly forward of the other three men. At a distance each patrol simultaneously became aware of each other and went to ground firing in each other's direction.

Schmeisser bullets hissed past me as I engaged them with my Tommy gun. The sound of each weapon is quite distinct.

The Tommy gun was my weapon of choice. It fired a heavier round which is big enough to stop an enemy in his tracks, and I had trained to be aware the ammunition carried by an infantryman is finite.

So the enemy patrol is ahead of me when suddenly a

Schmeisser opens up on my left. In the dark I could see little. I swivel my body to fire in this new direction, when I was about to press the trigger it dawned on me that the bullets are not coming in my direction, and suddenly remembered 'Charlie' Woodhouse favoured a Schmeisser. 'Charlie' never knew how near to death he became from one of his own men. The enemy patrol disengaged and much to our relief we found we had no casualties.

A concerted attack by 78th Division with just about everything thrown in and led by the 38th Irish Brigade made inroads on the German positions. The rain began to ease off and the one and only Bailey bridge which had been underwater so stopping movement across the Sangro re-appeared and was put into use. So a successful bridgehead became established despite desperate enemy counter attacks.

A report by Montgomery in a report to hand on the crossing of the Sangro, gives a thumbnail impression of the trials and tribulation the Brigade had experienced.

"In spite of continuous rain and acres of mud I managed to get a good bridge head over the Sangro, the trouble was to get my tanks and supporting weapons over, as the river was in flood and low level bridges merely disappeared. I took a good few risks. Twice I was pushed back to the river, once on my right and once on my left. But we came again and refused to admit it couldn't be done. The troops were quite magnificent, and in the most foul conditions you can ever imagine, the Sangro is normally about eighty feet wide and it became swollen to 300 feet and rose several feet, the water was icy cold as heavy snow fell in the mountains where the river rises. Many were drowned. Eventually we succeeded."

With the weather worsening further advances came to a halt. We were now over the Sangro, well established and required preparations before we would advance further. Winter had arrived with a vengeance. No substantial advances would be made now until spring arrived. Which meant winter would require continuous and extensive patrol work.

The 1st Surreys were withdrawn in December 1943 and were transported into the mountains for rest and recuperation to Frosolone. A few days later the rest of 78th Division moved back some sixty miles to Campobasso area, about twelve miles from Frasolone.

Campobasso was now the eighth army's leave centre. Formerly a holiday resort and a market town, it had three cinemas, Ensa (Entertainments National Service Association) theatre and clubs for officers and NCOs.

I was fortunate in having several days break in Campobasso but our time was cut short for after only a week we were moved higher into the mountain villages of Farah del Sangro, Castel Del Sangro and Aquarina, to command a spread out front of some ten miles of desolate sparsely occupied terrain overlooking the high parts of the river Sangro.

Most of the houses had been destroyed by the withdrawing Germans, but a few Italians, mostly the elderly, women and young children occupied some of the damaged houses. We were able to use a number of Italians as guides during the long cold, miserable hungry winter months for they had no love for the departed Germans who had made their hard existence much worse.

I remember Christmas Day of 1943/44. We had some decent food for a change and plenty to drink. The Battle Patrol got 'Charlie' Woodhouse if not drunk then very merry. The officers had made something of an officers mess in one of the houses, and I can still see an officer in the doorway urging a weaving Lt. John Woodhouse to "come and join us". "Come along, Jock, we are waiting for you." 'Jock' to his colleagues, John his true name and 'Charlie' to his patrol members. However he was addressed, he was a terrific, brave, and well liked officer who commanded respect.

Many patrols, some lasting three or four days in bitter cold snowy weather were carried out by the Battle Patrol. Apart from the awful energy-sucking weather we contended with erratic supplies of food. But good fortune smiled on us in the shape of the provision of wind-proof jackets, thick fleece, oiled socks and skis!

We were to be instructed in the art of skiing. 'Charlie' Woodhouse was an excellent skier and instructed us in the fine art of remaining upright on skis. The skis were Canadian and quite heavy. We spent hours rubbing resin into the undersides. A 'ski expert' was brought up to our group, but he only lasted a couple of days before he returned from whence he came, with 'frost bite'. We did several patrols on skis, being well aware the enemy had the advantage of being more expert practitioners. Fortunately we were not to run into enemy patrols whilst on skis.

We received information Germans were in the habit of visiting one of the isolated villages on the far side of the Sangro from their forward position in a house about half a mile to the rear of the village. Arrangements were made to take a full Battle Patrol into the area which was some distance away. We prepared for a patrol of several days, which required each man to carry his own food and extra ammunition. Lt. Woodhouse reminded us we would be in his (the Germans) area on the north side of the Sangro and as far as possible he was not to know of our existence. An Italian guide would lead us to the area.

Transport took us part of the way then it was a long walk and despite the cold weather we were soon sweating, loaded down as we were. When we finally got to the river and checked out the area, there were no surprises waiting for us, we crossed, up to our waists in icy cold water.

On the far side of the river the guide waited with Lt.

Woodhouse until all the Patrol crossed over. Reforming, we moved off along a track for a fair distance until we came to the ruins of Ateleta village. A few houses remained standing and in the darkness we were taken to one, where Italians made us welcome. With several of the patrol on guard outside, the remainder attempted to dry out in front of a roaring fire, the Italians stated the Germans never visited the village at night.

In daylight we moved away from the village and occupied an isolated house with half the patrol in ambush to be relieved by the other half several hours later. Like many of the Italian villages Ateleta was built on a hill requiring steps to the higher area. We had been informed the Germans occupied a position some half a mile away. Believed to be an observation unit of a dozen or so. The men were occasionally in the habit of visiting Ateleta in daylight.

The first day passed. No sign of any Germans, but on the second day two Germans, completely unaware of our men, appeared suddenly on the stepped roadway from a side street and started descending the steps.

A patrol man shouted "Hande Hoch!" (Hands up). One of the shocked men dropped his weapon and raised his hands. The other leapt to the side and tried to run but was shot and fell to the ground. The captured German was hustled away to the house we were occupying. The injured German lay dying on the steps. As we moved towards him several Italians ran out of a nearby house and tried to remove the wounded German's boots. We chased them away and carried the German to our house. We were to find he was 20 years old and was from Prussia. He had been hit in the chest and stomach. We did what we could for him but he died calling out for his mother. (Mutti!)

It was shortly after this incident I was to hear the bad news. The Battle Patrol was to be disbanded. It was felt that the men were getting exhausted by continual patrols; their expertise would be better served spread around the companies. Lt. Charlie Woodhouse was kind enough to give me a testimonial before he departed for another company. He was most upset about the disbandment.

We had done pretty well considering we were a small unit of only 14 men when at full strength. We had brought in a number of prisoners, been awarded several gongs and mentions and what was actually a surprising statistic, throughout that period we hadn't had a casualty. The latter comment was to be heavily endorsed in just a short period.

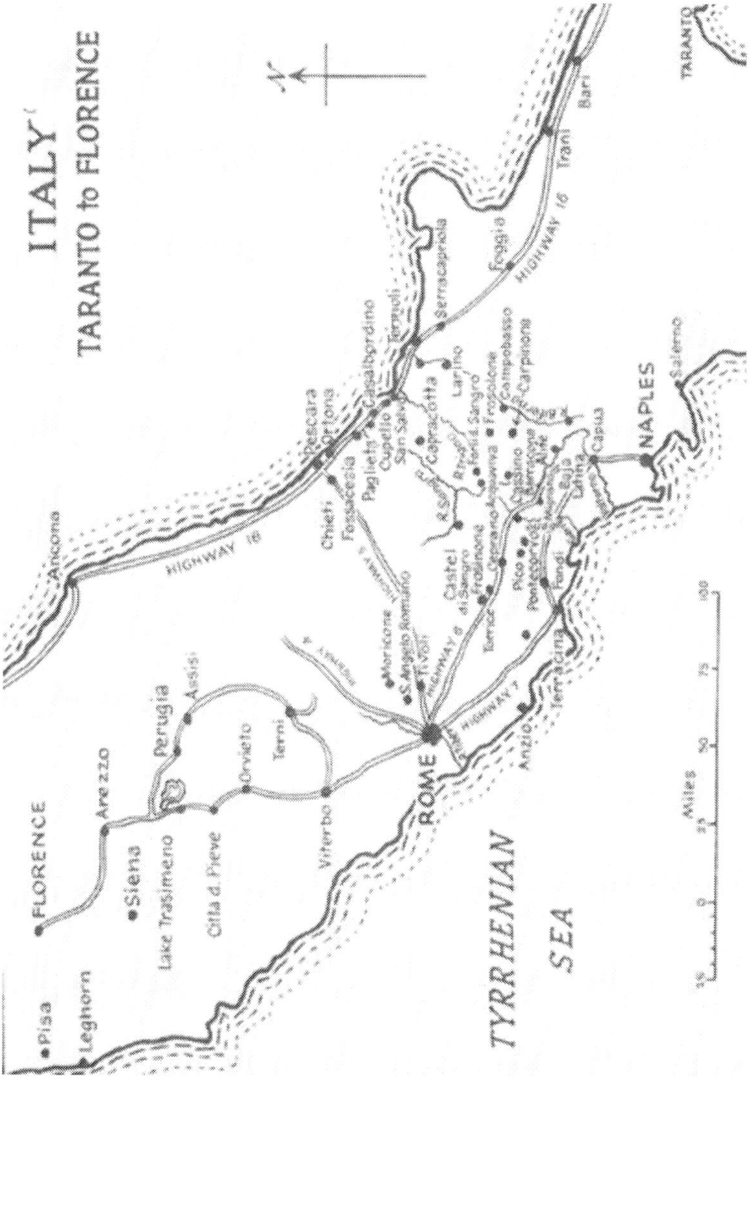
ITALY
TARANTO to FLORENCE
N
TYRRHENIAN
SEA
FLORENCE
Pisa
Leghorn
Siena
Arezzo
Lake Trasimeno
Citta d. Pieve
Perugia
Assisi
Orvieto
Terni
Viterbo
ROME
Tivoli
Anzio
Terracina
Ancona
Pescara
Ortona
Chieti
Foggia
Trani
Bari
TARANTO
NAPLES
Capua
Salerno
Serracapriola
HIGHWAY 16
HIGHWAY 6
HIGHWAY 7
Miles

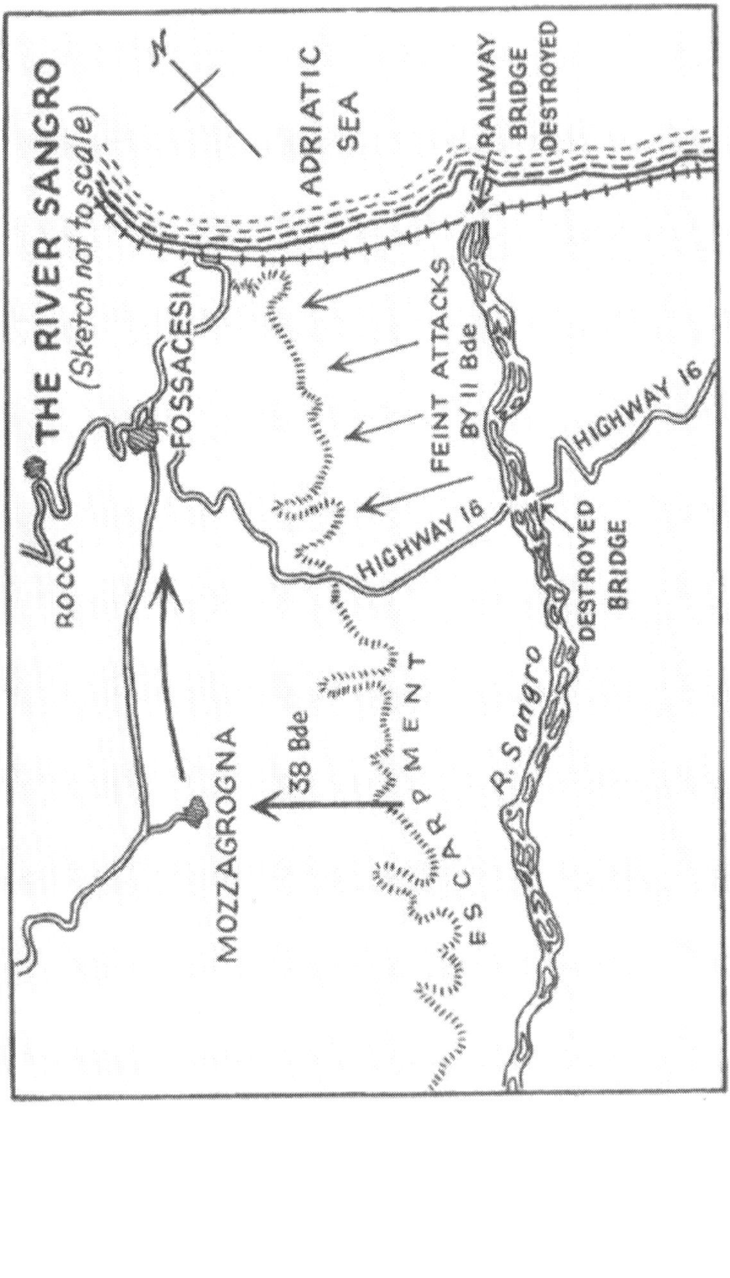

THE RIVER SANGRO
(Sketch not to scale)
N
ADRIATIC SEA
RAILWAY BRIDGE DESTROYED
ROCCA
FOSSACESIA
FEINT ATTACKS BY 11 Bde
HIGHWAY 16
HIGHWAY 16
DESTROYED BRIDGE
MOZZAGROGNA
38 Bde
ESCARPMENT
R. Sangro

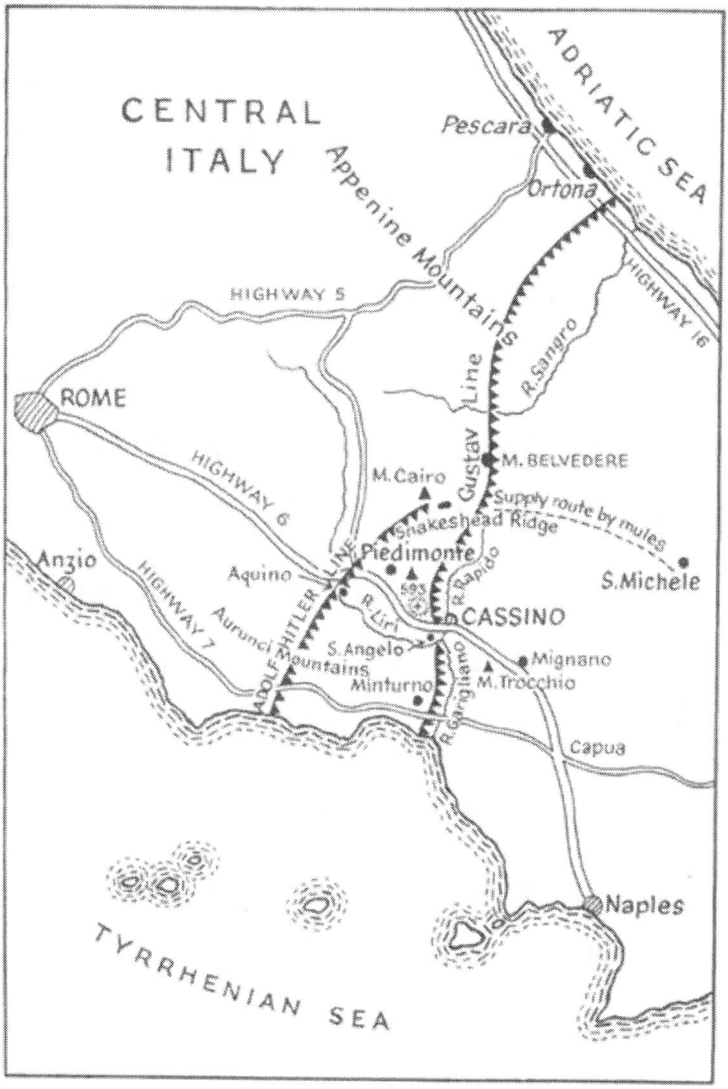
CENTRAL
ITALY
ADRIATIC SEA
Pescara
Ortona
Appenine Mountains
HIGHWAY 5
HIGHWAY 16
R. Sangro
Gustav Line
ROME
M. BELVEDERE
M. Cairo
HIGHWAY 6
Supply route by mules
Snakeshead Ridge
Piedimonte
S. Michele
Anzio
Aquino
593
R. Rapido
HIGHWAY 7
ADOLF HITLER LINE
R. Liri
CASSINO
Aurunci Mountains
S. Angelo
Mignano
Minturno
M. Trocchio
R. Garigliano
Capua
Naples
TYRRHENIAN SEA

ITALY
LAKE TRASIMENO
TO ARGENTA

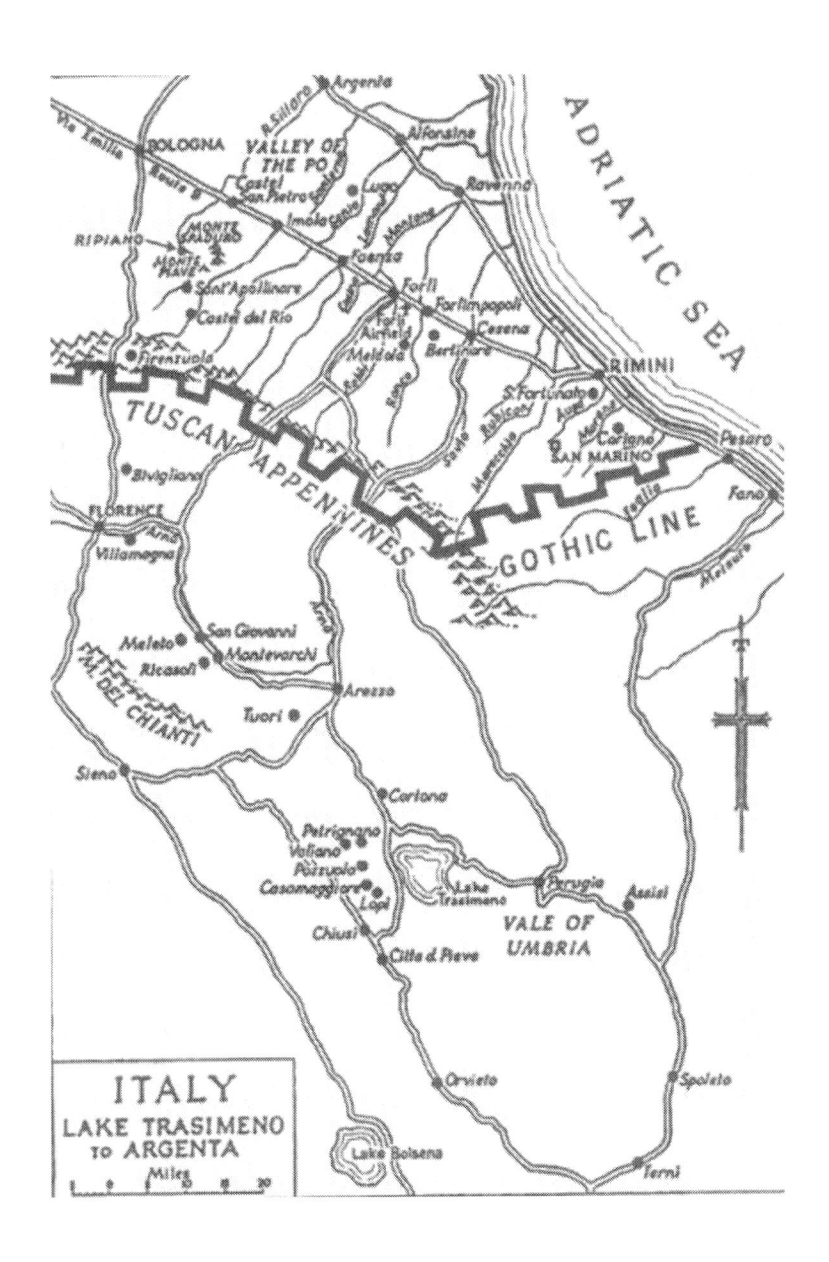

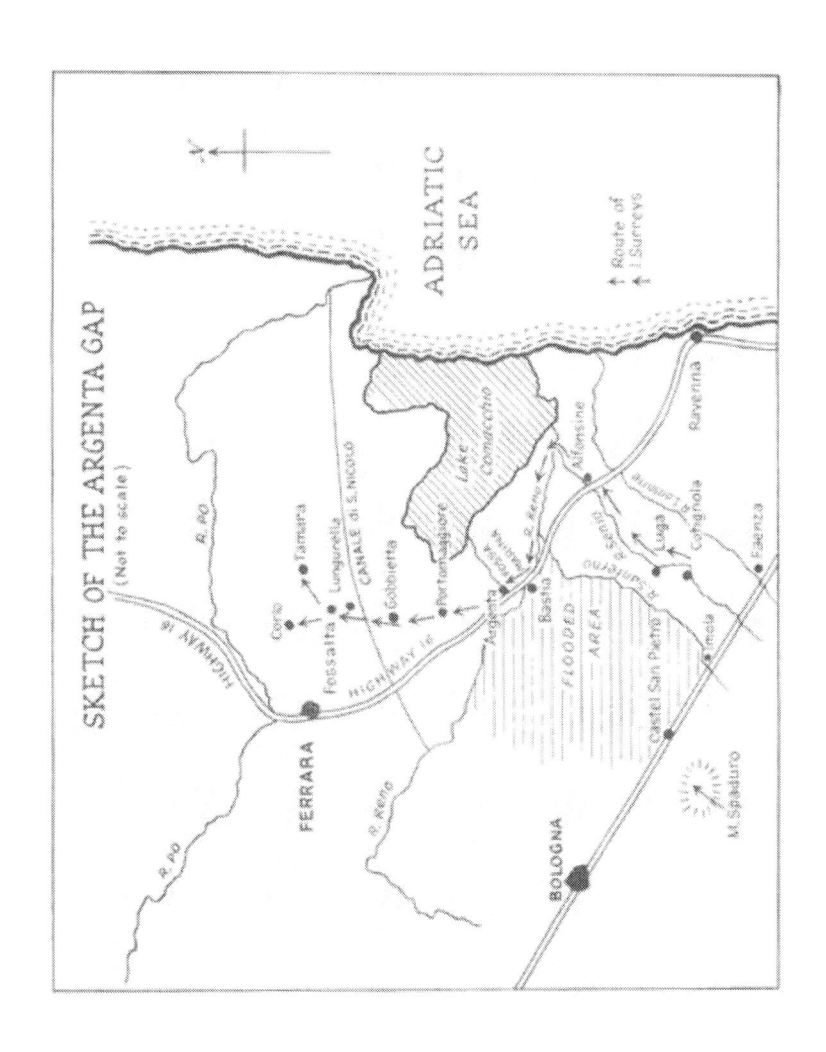

CHAPTER 8
BOMBING OF MONTE CASSINO

I returned to my old platoon. We were given the tricky job of anticipating a counter attack. Each night we moved forward to a group of slit trenches which were a few hundred yards from the Rapido. Throughout the night we would be watching and listening. Each night we would individually trek back to a farm building about four hundred yards to the rear where for one hour we would thaw out in front of the fire and have a bowl of soup made by two company cooks.

Just before daylight we moved back from the slit trenches, past the cookhouse and to a group of farm buildings. Here we made breakfast, cleaned kit and slept. After an evening meal we would return to the slit trenches for another night of discomfort.

One night the far left slit trench was over-run by an enemy patrol. The two men were taken prisoner. I reflected as a patrol man, it was a case of tit for tat.

It was here that I was, with another soldier, instructed to go forward from the trenches on one occasion to see if there were any signs of how and where the enemy might be crossing the river.

It was a pitch black night as we made our way silently to the edge of the river. My companion, who, like most infantry men, hated patrols was hyped up and nervy. At the river we carefully made our way along the shoreline. Here we came across what appeared to be wooden planks. Studying them I realised they could be joined together. We were probably looking at the makings of a footbridge. It was at this moment the enemy launched a barrage of mortar and machine gun fire. They did this unexpectedly and on a number of occasions, probably to deter any river crossing. I'd hit the ground at the first sound of rushing mortars. The barrage lasted only a few minutes. As the sound died away I stood up and looked around for my companion. No sign. For a moment I thought he may have been hit, but then realised that although noisy nothing had landed near us. After a short unsuccessful search I decided to return to my unit with what information we had.

It was scary. It dawned on me that the barrage may well have landed on or near the occupied slit trenches and if so the occupants would be pretty jittery and probably trigger happy. Any figure appearing out of the gloom from the direction of the river may well expect a dodgy reception.

As I neared the location of the slit trenches I started muttering "Don't shoot, I'm English" and repeated this continuously and with growing desperation as the trenches came into view. I stuck my arms in the air as I moved slowly forward.

The trenches were empty. Relief flooded through me. I was to discover the men had been pulled back in anticipation of an attack when the bombardment finished. It turned out my companion had managed to return earlier and was unscathed.

About this time I was to hear more bad news

The day after the break up of the Battle Patrol, John Woodhouse had accompanied his company commander Major Harvey on a patrol. Woodhouse knew the ground they were to traverse and took command of the patrol. They, with two men, were to look for places to bridge the river. Woodhouse should not have been with the group. He was supposed to be taking a rest.

With one soldier as leading scout they moved along a track for about 500 yards to a T-Junction. The scout stopped, and Woodhouse moved up to him. The scout whispered "there are some men there. I heard them". They listened for quite a while then Lt. Woodhouse decided to move on. The scout whose name was Pte. Vic James had only been in the Company two days. They moved on for another half mile or so, came out of the olive trees and onto the flood plain of the Rapido opposite Santa Angelo. A number of features were pointed out to Major Harvey and they returned in the direction of the T-Junction. The sides were mined so it was necessary to pass through the T-Junction.

As they closed on the junction a burst of firing and explosions blasted them. They hit the ground. Woodhouse had a German gun pushed into his back. He was lucky. The Germans were after prisoners. Pte Moody to the rear of Charlie had dived into the bushes and stayed still. Later he was able to return to the Surrey Lines. Major Harvey was killed in the ambush, his body found the following day. Also captured was Pte Vic James. For both, their war was over. The Germans returned to the north side of the Rapido with their captures by a boat crossing point at Santa Angelo. Ironically within 48 hours of the disbandment of the Battle Patrol its leader had been captured and a patrol had suffered casualties.

Dennis had been moved to another platoon and I was now in a forward position in the Monte Cassino area. To our rear was a depression in the side of the hill in which our headquarters and its functions such as cooks and supplies were located. With only a short distance between the enemy and ourselves, movement in daylight was suicidal particularly as the enemy was above us.

It was now around the middle of March. Finally the rain stopped. The day brightened. The allied bombers came.

The first wave came in high above Cassino. Then the

ground shook. For over 3 hours planes - Flying Fortresses and Liberators – over 500 of them, flying around in circles dropped bombs on Cassino. At the same time nearby targets were attacked and bombed by another 500 planes. No resistance in any form either by planes or ack ack fire was given by the enemy. It was a sight never to be forgotten. Hour after hour with no let up bombs rained down. The whole area was covered in dust and smoke. It appeared nothing could survive such an onslaught. But they did.

As the last of the bombs fell the New Zealanders attacked. They immediately ran into German infantry and paratroopers. Later it was discovered the Germans had been well prepared with re-enforced cellars and underground tunnels. The effect of the bombing, collapsed buildings and deep craters made the bringing up of artillery guns and tanks almost impossible. And the rain came again, turning the ground into a quagmire.

The gains made by the New Zealanders cost them dear with many casualties. If the attack had been successful our battalion with several others had been ready to move through and go forward through the Liri Valley. Other than patrols being carried out, the orders to move forward never came. Instead we were to be withdrawn back a distance and have a 4 day break.

It was 23/24 March when we marched four miles or so out of the line to a group of 3-ton trucks waiting to take us out to the rest camp. The night was dark, lit up by flashes from the guns. Some enemy shelling began with shells landing around us. With a group of men I climbed aboard one of the 3-tonners. We were on a built up road. Each side the road fell away into blackness. We had hardly moved away when a blinding light seemed to hit us. The truck was blown sideways and fell off the made up road crashing down onto its side. Inside the truck men hurtled into each other. My face hit a stanchion supporting the canvas cover and I blacked out. Next thing I knew I was being pulled out of the wreckage. Several of the men had bad injuries. One, I recall, had a broken back.

The side of my face had swollen and my teeth felt loose. With others I was evacuated first to 2nd General Hospital and after an x-ray of my face onto 104 General Hospital. These details are in a diary I kept and occasionally completed. I had a bath and soft food. Once again I was moved further to the rear, to Barleta via Naples, to the 93rd General Hospital.

It was on the hospital train nearing Naples that I had the good fortune to see a most amazing sight, the eruption of the volcano Vesuvius. It was, creating a giant cauliflower of billowing smoke rising twice as high as the clouds. It was a truly unique sight, especially for a London lad.

It appeared I had a fractured jaw, moving it was painful and difficult. I was given cocoa and grapefruit juice through a straw and later specially prepared food.

I was in hospital for several weeks before my face healed. Finally I was given the okay to depart and return to my unit. As I was leaving I met up with another soldier also departing the hospital. "Hi," I said as we walked, "How are things?" "Could be better," he replied. He then told me his reason for his hospital visit. It transpired he had, during a drunken evening had a session with a woman who charged for her services. Not only did she give him her services but – as he put it to me - "I caught a dose"!

The soldier looked downcast and I realised why, when he then said "And I'm married!" I thought about his predicament. "Well if you've been treated maybe she doesn't need to know" I said. In those days treatment of V.D was not to the standards now available. Horror stories of the treatment - including the use of the 'umbrella' were bandied about.

Venereal Disease was considered to be a self-inflicted act punishable by loss of pay. I grasped his problem when he said "She will know something is up when they stop the marriage allowance." When I departed I wished him good luck. We both appreciated he was really in need, of some.

CHAPTER 9
SAILOR UNCLE BILL & MONKEY

We were resting up in a quiet area, acting as a reserve company, the Section sitting or sprawled around in a rough circle just chewing the fat. One of the men had been talking about a relative in the peacetime navy who had had a lucky escape from some situation or other. As he finished his account the men fell silent, mulling over on what they had heard. It seemed to me the atmosphere needed lightening. "I've got an uncle who is in the Merchant Navy", I began. "Whether he is alive or dead I haven't a clue. The last time I remember seeing him was when I was a kid and he turned up with this monkey on his shoulder." With faces now turned towards me, I continued. "We were living in Battersea at the time, I must have been about ten or eleven. One day there's a knock on the door, my mother opens it to see a big burly guy with a wide smile, wearing a naval peaked cap, in blue, and sitting on his shoulder is a tiny rhesus monkey. "Hello Minnie". It's her brother Bill, a merchant seamen home from his travels. We had another Uncle named Bill and so this character was known to us kids as Sailor Uncle Bill.

So Sailor Uncle Bill, a lovely cheerful man who is virtually a stranger to us kids – me and my two brothers – makes himself at home with his kid sister and my Dad. Of course we are all fascinated by this tiny monkey. My mother wasn't best pleased to be told that Sailor Uncle Bill had named the monkey after his sister, "Minnie"!

Now in those days entertainment for adults seemed to be based on having a few drinks at their favourite drinking house. So that evening, being at the weekend, the grown-ups go to their normal drinking pub, the 'CDS'. "The what?" asked one of the circle, puzzled. "I can't remember the actual name of the pub, in fact I've never heard it called anything other than the CDS, after the Publican whose name is – or was, Charlie Smith". I stopped for a moment, then, "It's in York Road, Battersea. All my Aunts and Uncles seemed to meet there." Seeing a few nods of understanding, I continued.

"So anyway, my Mum, Dad and Sailor Uncle Bill with "Minnie" sitting on his shoulder – it's got a little leather collar and a strap fixed to Sailor Uncle Bill's jacket – head for the pub. When they enter the bar, us kids stand outside in the sort of foyer glimpsing what goes on in the bar each time the door swings open. Mum comes out with a soft drink for us and a square biscuit each, the sort you can only nibble round the edges as it's as hard as a brick.

Inside the bar the monkey is of course the centre of attraction and Sailor Uncle Bill is holding forth on where its from and advising the more intrepid punters that although small "Minnie' has been known to bite.

Standing at the bar with a freshly drawn pint of ale and surrounded by interested drinkers and letting "Minnie" take sips from his beer, Sailor Uncle Bill is in his element. Suddenly "Minnie" stands up on Bill's shoulder and with his tiny hand gripping onto Sailor Uncle Bill's hair pees with abandon. He pees across the bar over the bartenders bald head as he is drawing a glass of beer and part of the assembled throng is sprayed with pungent urine some of which drops into beer glasses. Pandemonium! The drinkers who have not been in the line of fire are doubled up with laughter at the sight of dripping wet irate punters who are now yelling obscenities at the man with a monkey on his shoulder.

My parents are in the fortunate position of being untouched by the pee. The red faced barman mopping his bald pate with a bar towel is bawling above the noise for

Sailor Uncle Bill to get out of the pub. "And take that bloody animal with you and don't come back!"

"Back home on hearing what had happened us kids thought it hilarious as did, finally my parents". I looked around at the grinning soldiers. "The following weekend it was decided that the visit to the pub would be without "Minnie" who had surprisingly been on good behaviour all week. Mum and her brother left out some food and water and secured "Minnie" with his lead. "Minnie" watched all this palaver with his bright shiny eyes and didn't seem bothered as his owner headed for the door. (I say 'his' ' cos despite his cheeky name it was actually a male monkey). At the pub apologies were made and pints paid for those who alleged they were in the 'firing line' and peace established, until we returned home.

Entering the room we were faced with an unforgettable sight. Somehow "Minnie" had found a way of loosening his strap and had created mayhem, what with wallpaper torn from the walls, and cushions ripped and feathers everywhere, pictures off the walls, his bowl of water upturned and himself perched on the back of an armchair chattering with presumable anger at being left alone!" I grinned. "It was then mum spotted her favourite armchair was wet – and not with water!"

One of the soldiers said, "What happened next?" "Well," I replied. "My Dad didn't say much, but mum said, between her teeth, "so when were you thinking of leaving?"

Sailor Uncle Bill took the hint. "We will be off first thing tomorrow morning back to my ship." And that was the last we saw of Sailor Uncle Bill and "Minnie" the monkey! Mum threw out the saturated armchair, but the personal fragrance of "Minnie" the monkey lingered on – and not only in the memory!

Sometime around this time, my group were resting up in a small town. For a few days we were enjoying 'R&R' (Rest and Recuperation). One evening a guy dropped into our small group. We were just chewing the fat and supping wine. "Found a woman who's on the game." He sounded excited. "I ain't had a shag for ages, anybody here up for it with me?" The merits and demerits of the subject were debated. Perhaps the wine had flowed too freely, for a while. Later my drinking partners heaved themselves to their feet. I hadn't moved. Benny (I'll call him Benny) put down his bottle of wine as he stood up, peering at me, asked "Ain't you coming, Reg?" "Not yet he ain't," grinned a wag. It was a cause of merriment. "Sure." I got to my feet. "Where does this woman hang out?"

We moved off into the darkness and followed our informant. I had no intention of taking up any sexual services on offer, but I wasn't about to tell my companions. I had a reputation to consider! Maybe I was under-sexed. Much more likely was the memory of a sad married soldier exiting from the V.D. hospital department I'd met sometime earlier.

In the gloom the soldier pointed. "That's it." A small building isolated from the collection of nearby houses came into view.

Lit by a spluttering oil lamp the bare walls enclosed the one room into which we filed. In the corner a built-up area with cooking pots indicated a kitchen of sorts. A small table and two wooden forms provided the bulk of the furniture. Above our heads a timbered floor had been constructed across roughly half the area. A home built ladder provided access.

A woman in her late thirties rose to greet us. Her body was moving to thickness particularly at the waist. She may have been pretty at one time but sadness now blurred her features. "Buona sera," she greeted.

You could say I only had an academic interest in the actions of my colleagues as one by one with a measurable period in between they followed each other up the ladder. When the last had pulled his braces back on and climbed down to earth with a self-conscious smirk I nodded towards the door. "You guys needn't wait for me." Benny looked surprised. `` I want to practice my Italian- afterwards." My emphasis on the last word raised a grin and the guys shuffled out into the darkness.

I climbed the ladder. A typical heavy wooden Italian bed took up most of the floor space. My eyes studied the area, across and against the wall stood a chest of some sort, beside the bed a hard seated chair. She sat with her back against the head board. I sat with my back against the hard chair. "Quanto Costa, Signorina?" she quoted the fee she charged. I placed the lira on the bed in front of her and as she prepared to move I waved and indicated it was unnecessary. She looked confused. In bad Italian I explained that instead of any coupling, I would prefer five minutes of her time in conversation. This way my friends would assume that I had done the deed. She still looked confused but began to relax as I continued in my bad Italian.

I asked her if she was from the local community. She shook her head, named a village some distance away the name of which I have long forgotten. Briefly her story explained the sadness on her face. A poor background to start with, she had married an equally poor son of a farmer who had been called into the Italian army, he had been killed leaving her with two children. Money was scarce. Thus she did what she did. With no one around to see how soft I was, I placed on the bed cover my remaining lira, wished her well, and departed.

We came across a bag of white flour in a deserted farmhouse. There was a discussion as to whether it was really consumable. Several of the section stuck a finger in it and tasted it. It had the word 'farina' on the package. After it was confirmed it was indeed flour we discussed what we could do with it. "We could make a Plum Duff with it, or Spotted Dick" I suggested. Following many rude and ribald remarks about alternatives I found I was nominated to make a pudding with it. I wasn't too certain how one made a Plum Duff but came to the conclusion it shouldn't be too difficult, and set too, whilst the men were engaged elsewhere. Mixing the flour with a lump of margarine, sugar, water and some jam and into something resembling a white soft ball and with water bubbling merrily in the biscuit tin, it dawned on me I needed a cloth or something to wrap it in. Mentally I reviewed what was available. The only thing I could come up with which was clean, large enough and available was a pair of army underpants that I had been recently issued with following a visit to the mobile bath unit. I inspected them. Unused, with a sort of off white khaki colour and certainly roomy enough they seemed to be just the job. Wrapped and tightly tied I popped the concoction into the boiling water. I found I had to keep refilling the container several times as the water evaporated. I guessed it would need several hours of boiling and fielded the occasional enquiries of "Is it ready yet?" with "Give it time"!

    Finally I concluded it had had long enough. Untying the 'cooking cloth' I revealed a pudding which reminded me of a cannonball but that looked good enough to eat. And when the men returned from their labours, plopped pieces into proffered mess tins. Surprisingly the verdict was pretty good but there were a number of comments that it had a soapy taste. I had kept the 'cooking cloth' out of sight and decided there was no point in sharing information on the culinary use of my khaki coloured underpants.

CHAPTER 10
FOURTH CASSINO BATTLE

We commenced training in river crossings. The weather became hot and now instead of mud everywhere it rapidly dried out and turned into dust.

The final battle for Cassino began in the middle of May'44. The Royal Engineers managed to build three Bailey Bridges over the River Rapido and the Allied Forces obtained a Bridgehead. 78th (Battleaxe) Division's task including the 1st Battalion, the East Surreys was to surge forward, by-pass Cassino and despite enemy resistance advance to Highway 6 the only road which would give access to the Liri Valley and to the North and Rome. The area was perfect defence country for this time of the year, trees and bushes were flush with thick green leaves which provided good cover for enemy ambushes and snipers. The Germans had also built defensive positions of mines, pill boxes and other obstacles making the advances extremely hazardous. Shelling from both sides was continuous and dust billowed as tanks moved ever forward supporting the waves of attacking infantry.

Finally the Battleaxe Division broke through to the Liri Valley and Highway 6. About the same time the Poles succeeded in finally capturing the Cassino Monastery despite their high number of casualties.

At last, at the fourth attempt and with great cost to both sides the problem of Monte Cassino and the town of Cassino had been dealt with and the road to Rome was now open.

The Germans began a full scale withdrawal but leaving rear-guards to delay the advance of our troops. 78th (Battleaxe) Division including our Battalion joined in the advance.

In the early days of June 1944 the American Armed Force with General Clark had entered Rome, which had been declared an open city. Forty-eight hours later the allied invasion of Europe, D-Day, began.

Our Brigade, now on motor transport passed through Rome and stayed in the north of the city for a short while, before moving forward again towards Lake Trasimeno. Here enemy resistance stiffened with more German Divisions being brought down from the North. A number of sorties and patrols were carried out and casualties increased, particularly in the area of Citta Della Preve.

A major attack by 8th Army was now required to breach the enemy's defences at Lake Trasimeno. The Surreys with other Battalions of the 11th Brigade made gains slowly along the western side of the lake, often held up by heavy machine gun fire.

On 1 July the Brigade was relieved and moved back to Panicarola further south and the rest of the 78th (Battleaxe) Division centred on the Sabine Hills a few miles from Rome. At this time I was able to make a visit to Rome. Our only previous visit was throughout the night as we were in pursuit of the enemy.

The Division was now being pulled out of the line in preparation for an overdue long rest to be taken in Egypt. And so, a day before my birthday on the 11th July 1944, the Battalion entrained and moved south past the ruins of Cassino finally arriving at Taranto. We embarked on the liner Britannic heading for Port Said. After ten days of enjoyable weather we reached Egypt. Here we stayed in a tented camp in the Suez Canal zone for several weeks having rest and training before moving to near Mena on the outskirts of Cairo in sight of the Pyramids and the Sphinx. I had the great fortune of being able to visit one of the pyramids during my time here. I had the strange impression and a feeling of disappointment when I first saw the famous site. The pyramid seemed to be smaller than I had always imagined. It was then I realised this impression was caused by the fact no other building is there to make a comparison. It is only when nearing, the size of the blocks of shaped stone one upon another that one appreciated the way it rises into a blue cloudless sky.

Another wrong impression I had carried for many years was that the pyramid and been built above the Royal incumbent those thousands of years ago. I was to discover my error when, having paid a small fee to the resident Arab, he conducted me into the interior. I was shown how the casket was inched up slowly towards the room at the apex of the pyramid. Here I was shown a hollowed out massive piece of stone- reminding me of a huge bath- in which the Pharaoh had reposed. I also remember thick around the heavy edges of the tomb was solidified candle grease caused by the many visitors.

It was during this sojourn whilst in the Suez Canal Zone I can remember standing on the deck of a ship, sailing along the centre of the canal clad only in khaki shorts, brown as a local and sporting a red tasseled fez. How it came about I can no longer recall! But I do remember a dance square being laid for the pleasure of the officers to dance upon at Mena.

An officer's entertainment evening with female nurses and the like from Cairo and music provided by a military band. The cement patch also had the pleasure of the members of the Sgt's mess enjoying its use, before the dance floor was smashed up and removed out of sight. The lower ranks 'volunteered' to provide the waiter service....

We were able to take leave in Cairo and visited other

Egyptian cities. One visit stays in the mind. Several of us stayed at the Spitfire Club, a small cheap hotel at, I believe, Alexandria. On our first day we had a meal when we booked in before leaving to visit the sights. The Egyptian running the place seemed overwhelmed by the sudden influx of guests and certainly lacked sufficient staff. Later that day having been shown our bedrooms and getting ready to turn in, I realised there was no sheet on my bed. On pointing this out to the proprietor who seemed completely out of his depth, he assured me he would deal with it, if I would kindly wait in the room below.

The proprietor returned, smiling and rubbing his hands together and assured me the matter had now been dealt with.

On returning to my room I undressed and pulling the bedclothes back and about to get into bed when I spied the sheet. There was something familiar about it. Small dried reddish marks formed a pattern. Further inspection confirmed my suspicions. My "sheet" had been the tablecloth on the table when we had eaten earlier!

Another enjoyment we were able to have was to take the short journey to Heliopolis and join the many nationalities making use of the large open air swimming pool and the local facilities, when our duties allowed.

Due to the transfer of a number of army formations from Italy to France where the main events were now taking place and the unexpected tough resistance of the Germans at the Gothic Line, the Division's promised long rest was suddenly cut short and it was required to immediately return to Italy.

It so happened that I was undergoing treatment for a problem in both eyes at this time. I had been hospitalised for my sight was being affected so much so that I had difficulty in identifying objects. The infection was probably caused, said the doctor, by the water in the Heliopolis swimming pool being infected by female urine. (in actual fact the doctor identified a particular nationality which it is unnecessary for me to mention.)

So the Division with the East Surreys was long gone when I was discharged, my sight fully restored.

I was in a transit camp with other men awaiting shipment back to Italy. For a number of days we hung about until half a dozen of us infantry men, all dischargers from hospital, were told to be ready to embark. It turned out that a cargo ship the Samcebo was due to sail to Famagusta, Italy, and we were to act as security guards aboard. The Samcebo, we were to find, was one of the infamous SAM ships built in America by a Mr. Kaiser. I say 'infamous' because they were built without rivets and had a reputation for breaking their backs in bad weather. Never the less they did a good job of transporting goods to many countries. Fortunately the weather was good during our journey. This didn't stop me listening to the incessant creaking of the welded plates whilst lying in my hammock at night.

The journey provided one or two incidents of interest. We pulled in near the port of Syracuse. Unable to get closer to the shore a wooden platform was secured to the landward side of the ship and goods off loaded by the ship's crane. Our little clique of soldiers took advantage of the platform to fish but with little success, although we could see them moving near the platform edges. We were thus engaged when a soldier spied a much bigger object close to the platform. "Shark!" he yelled, retreating hurriedly from the edge. The shark didn't seem to be in any sort of hurry cruising round the timbers. It was then I made my personal claim to fame! Picking up a boat hook I whacked the intruder across the back of its head as it rose up near the surface! It didn't seem bothered but it moved leisurely out to sea!

It didn't take us long to realise that some of the unloaded goods were never going to reach a military destination. On going ashore we soon found the Mafia had things well organised. In a covered area army supplies of goods, mostly clothing were being exchanged for cash in a business-like manner. Prices were firm and there was no bartering. In the holds of the Samcebu were underwear, trousers, jackets, socks and so on in addition to heavier material. We found an almost casual attitude to this 'black market'. So we tried to out for ourselves. Putting on several army vests under out uniforms we went ashore and entered the building. Half a dozen tables each serviced by a couple of locals were before us. We stripped off, folded the vests, replaced our jackets, and handed over the goods. A quick check of the number of items by a swarthy local and cash was handed over.

We headed for a bar and sat with glasses of vino discussing the events of the evening. Now we soldiers, incidentally mostly infantry men and only half a dozen of us on the 'Samcebu", were no angels and were prepared to pick up some easy money as the next man. But the fact many of the items were supposedly bound for our troops in Italy, didn't sit well with us. From what we could see of things quite a few people knew what was going on. So it was decided that only if we went ashore for the evening, would take a few vests with us to pay for the evening's entertainment. So with our conscience allayed by somewhat doubtful morals this is what we did for the period it took to unload the ship.

After a few days the Samcebu continued its journey finally arriving at Taranto where , we, its passengers disembarked and after some confusion and delay were finally bussed to a transit camp where we were to await return to our respective battalions.

I was moved to a transit camp to wait return to unit. It was here that my life took on a change of direction. Also the chip on my shoulder got me into trouble again.

Although I was back into routine infantry life – firing on the range, square bashing and the like – I found we had plenty of time off. We were in the camp awaiting re-posting back to our regiments but everything seemed to move at a slow pace.

I met up with another East Surrey lad, whose nick-name was 'Happy', which associated nicely with his surname Hope. He was, as his nick name suggested an easy going character, up for anything. Although he lived in Brighton on the coast, he hailed originally from London.

We became experts at dodging parades and giving ourselves an easy life. After parade hours there were a lot of card playing groups. Also Housey Housey, horse racing betting and so on. Happy and I joined in with gusto. The trouble was we were lousy pickers of horses and the same with Pontoon or Card Brag. We didn't enjoy being broke all the time so we devised ways of earning a few bob. I suppose purists would see it as "black market' activity, but the thought didn't cross our minds. We were hard up and wanted to play more pontoon. So we'd buy a dozen packs of toothpaste and go into town and sell it to the locals. On each we made a nice profit. After a while we found the locals had all the toothpaste they wanted. We had to re-think our selling tactics. We found that tooth brushes were, compared with the white stuff that went on them, in short supply. So we cornered the market. The Italians were very keen to buy toothbrushes, and we were happy to provide them. But there was a proviso. We made it a condition that if they wanted a toothbrush they had to also buy six tubes of toothpaste. The cash came in nicely and we were back at the gambling tables- and still losing.

From the locals we were having continual requests for cigarettes. Happy didn't smoke so we decided that we would become suppliers of the tobacco weed. This increased our income. Now, these activities and others of a similar nature were, as you would imagine, frowned upon by officialdom. A guard room at the gate was sometimes a problem in the transfer of 'goods'. Searches and stop checks were the norm. Nobody was allowed out with a pack. We started to wear overcoats. They had large pockets. It was on a nightly trip out that we were stopped in a check at the gate. I had 200 cigarettes in overcoat pockets and Happy had the same. We were put on a charge and remanded to appear in front of the officer commanding the following morning.

We were smartly marched before the officer and the charge read out. On the desk before us were the confiscated cigarettes. When asked what I had to say I protested my and my friend's innocence. The reason we were carrying cigarettes in such quantities, I said, was to keep them safe. I said on occasions in the past when we went out to town to partake in local beverages we would return to our tent to find all our cigarettes stolen. The only safe way to keep them was on our person.

The captain looked at me silently for a long time, saying nothing. Then he sighed and said "Cambridge. This time I'll give you the benefit of doubt. Don't come in front of me again! Give them back their cigarettes." With that we were marched out. We celebrated by going out the following evening with our pockets full of cigarettes, returning with empty pockets and a roll of cash.

On another occasion we were caught with ten bars of soap. Once again we were remanded to appear before the Company Commander. This could become a nuisance. If we got C.B. (Confined to Barracks) our spending money could be affected.

We hit on a plan of action. The evening before we were charged we were quite busy. The next morning we went through the usual procedure of appearing before the Company Commander.

As usual the charge was read out. We were asked if we had anything to say. Once again I made myself the chief spokesman. "Sir", I said, "We are not guilty as charged. It had not been our intention to sell the bars of soap. We had arranged to exchange them with a local friend for candles as we have no light in the tent and I was unable to read a book I wanted to read." The captain said, "What a load of tosh. You know you're not allowed to have a naked light in a tent."

"But Sir, we knew we weren't allowed a naked light. We have taken precautions."

The captain leaned back in his chair "What do you mean, you have taken precautions?"

"We have compo tins with holes in the side with wire handles. We put half a candle in the tin, light it and its quite safe, Sir."

The officer called in his orderly. "Go to this solder's tent and bring me any compo tins with holes knocked in them." The soldier salutes smartly and disappeared. "If he comes back empty handed you are for the high jump!"

The orderly returned with 4 smoke blackened cans. Placing them on the table he saluted and vanished. The captain looked at the tins, looked at the Sgt-major standing to our rear. "Case dismissed" he said. Then to me he said "Your luck's run out. Do not come before me again!"

Whilst at the transit camp I had the good fortune to get a pass to Naples which was no great distance from the camp.

Naples in those war torn days, and maybe still, is a place of extremely old houses, narrow streets, forbidding alleyways and dismal lighting. It had a secretive air despite its drinking houses and its occasional bursts of laughter from behind closed doors. I am of course giving my impression which remains solidly in my mind. Yet I also remember a most attractive imposing building which if my memory is correct was a royal palace, which had been "given over" to the allied cause as a glorified NAAFI tea house. There was a notice to be read as one entered, not to deface or damage the walls. The most beautiful and astounding historic work of art covered the walls and ceilings. It was breathtaking. To me, with no knowledge of art, artists or painters of any generation it created an unforgettable impression (angels and religious symbols).

Came the evening, myself and a guy from my company who I palled up with on the truck to Naples who I got to know as Freddie, wandered into the narrow streets and finished up in a bar filled with servicemen of all nations. It was hot, noisy and a cheerful escape from our normal or more accurately abnormal lives.

The vino flowed and we were merrily drunk when we finally hit the streets. Following us were a couple of Canadians also full of bonhomie who we had spoken to earlier. In the darkness we four stood unsteadily making our minds up where to go next. "I wanna woman," one of the Canadians said drunkenly. "You don't wanna woman," rejoined his mate. "I wanna woman," repeated the first Canadian and lurched off in the direction of pin points of light in the distance. We followed unsteadily. We were now in the red light district. A door opened and two women waved us in and as we sat on rickety chairs poured each of us a glass of wine. I looked around drunkenly trying to see things clearly. It was a poverty stricken room. I made out a bed, a table, a hob and not much else.

The wine tasted rough on the tongue. A mixture of

broken English, some Italian and descriptive hand movements confirmed the Canadian's requirements and the elder of the two ladies confirmed the transaction by quoting a price which was agreed by the gentleman in question after a short period of haggling. We, the audience, seated, wine sodden looked on owlishly. Handing the agreed fee to the younger of the women, who promptly passed it over to the older woman, the Canadian, about to move towards the bed on which the woman was now seated, stopped suddenly, turned, and pointing to us said "I don't want an audience!" he had trouble with the last word. The older woman finally grasped what he was on about, urged us to our feet and indicated we should enter a small room off to the side, access to which was provided by a door which had seen better days. The wood had splits and cracks where the dry air over the years had shrunken the timber.

The woman ushered us through the door. Seeing our reluctance she held up two fingers and said "Due Momento," and closed the door. In the darkness we faced the door. Through the cracks we were able to watch the performance as the Canadian's backside rose and lowered, we could see the older woman's back as she rinsed glasses in the corner sink. Freddie, with his eye to a hole in the door, giggled, "Seems to be enjoying it" he said. Our Canadian sighed, seemingly sobering up. "He's bloody stupid. He's already had treatment for gun." I was baffled. It was not a phrase I'd heard. "Gonorrhea" he muttered.

We stood there in darkness, silent, as this information was absorbed. The door was opened and we filed back into the room as the soldier 'adjusted his dress' to use a phrase, Freddie and I regained our seats. The Canadians decided to move on but we indicated we would finish our drinks. It was time to split from the Commonwealth boys.

The older woman now offered the younger woman's

services to us. We declined. I thought it was only fair to let the women know of the situation. In broken Italian I told them the soldier had been 'sick' in the past with a contagious condition. When they grasped what I was trying to tell then their reaction was immediate. With shrill voices they berated us for not warning them earlier, not understanding we were also unaware, then the older woman placed a metal bowl of water on a chair into which she shook a pink powder which she stirred vigorously speaking in anguished rapid Italian ceaselessly. The tearful younger woman approached the chair, pulled up her dress and was treated by her companion on her intimate parts in front of two open mouthed soldiers, who decided the time had come to depart.

CHAPTER 11
THE COMMANDOS & BACK TO BLIGHTY

It was during this period a call was made for volunteers to join the Army Commandos. The campaign in Italy was on its last legs and the intention of the Commandos was to prepare for action in the Far East against the Japanese.

Now, in 1941 I had volunteered to join the Commandos but had been rejected as "undesirable" due to the fact I had just returned from the 'Military Correction Establishment' at Dundee.

On the day the interviews took place I, with a number of other potential volunteers waited outside a tent until individually we were called in to be confronted by an officer and several senior NCOs.

Questioning was direct and to the point. I had a feeling things weren't going so well and suspected I was about to be turned down when I had a brain wave. From my tunic pocket I pulled out the testimonial 'Charlie' Woodhouse had given me on the disbanding of the Battle Patrol and offered it in evidence of my good character. The atmosphere seemed to change and I was asked detailed questions of actions in which I had been involved. The officer then said I could join the group of those accepted for training but pointed out the take up of acceptances were quite low. I knew the training was going to be very tough. How tough, I was soon to find out. Happy and my other friends said they preferred a quieter life but wished me luck.

With my kit packed I boarded the truck with 12 or so men. We were heading for the Commando training camp at a place I believe was called Monteforti somewhere in the mountains.

On a long straight hilly road the truck came to a halt. Instructors appeared. With shouts and threats we were instructed to de-buss. Pointing up the road the chief instructor said "the camp is ten miles away." He looked at his watch and uttered a time which I've now forgotten. "At that time the gate will be closed and late arrivals will be put back on the truck and RTU (returned to unit)" he said "start running."

Off we went. The ground was hilly and the day was hot. The group began spacing out. It became obvious a number were not going to make it. I found it hard going but was determined. I got my second wind and kept pace with the leading men. I suppose half or so of the chaps made it. Some gave up running and others were too slow. With some minutes to spare I managed to be inside the gate when it clanged shut.

First hurdle over. Much more was to come. Thank God I was pretty fit. Jumping off the rear of moving trucks, crossing rivers hanging onto equipment, unarmed combat, 'enemy' exercises, and speed walking distances – you made it or you were facing RTU.

Finally, unlike a number of unfortunates, I was awarded my green beret and issued with a fighting knife. I was now a fully-fledged Commando, a member of No2 Commando of Special Services Brigade.

The Brigade was for a period of several weeks used as infantry in the line. I didn't know it at the time but we were about to carry out an operation which was to be, apart from anything else pretty exhausting. Just north of Ravena is Commachio lagoon. It is separated from the Adriatic by a strip of land, a desolate area, swampy and not at all pleasant. The enemy occupied the strip with most of its troops south of the canal which connected the lake to the Adriatic Sea. Our Commando was to cross the lagoon to the north of 9 Commando. We also needed to cross a dyke, a mess of thick mud and wooden stakes, and take 2 bridges. Information on the depth and size of the lagoon was scarce. Locals said it was impractical to cross it and it hadn't ever been crossed. When the time came to carry out the assault, it soon became clear there were real problems with the crossing. The level of water was unexpectedly low and had receded leaving thick glutinous mud. Some boats were just too cumbersome to handle. The assault boats despite their weight were pulled and pushed through this mud nearly a mile in the dark. It took several hours but finally we reached deeper water and the boats could float. Eventually we made it to the far side. Amazingly the enemy, whose positions faced a different direction, as they considered it impossible for an attack to come from such an unlikely location and were receiving a barrage from our artillery, were completely surprised. The bridges were captured. An assault on the enemy was successful and by the following evening the Brigade had consolidated it positions. Out tanks managed to use a bridge to cross over Lake Commachio and we moved forward and continued forcing the enemy back. Later we were to be relieved. About 1000 prisoners were made prisoners of war and the enemy had a high number of casualties. The Commando Brigade suffered its own losses. My overriding memory of this whole period is of black greasy mud, more stinking mud and wooden stakes rising from the smelly blackness like crosses for the lost.

Near Argenta No 43 (Royal Marine) Commandos and 2 Commando finally drove the enemy from the wet area south west of the town, other troops of 5th Corps drove through the Argenta gap and the war for Italy was over.

It had been my last battle in Italy. Sometime later I was to find my old pal Dennis Scaife had been wounded and captured. The next time I met him was in England. I was then to hear that Eric Monsey had been killed, just days before the end of the war in Italy. Years later I discovered it was at a place in one of the final battles of the war. He was buried in the cemetery, at Argenta.

2 Commando now returned to England where we disembarked at Southampton. As we sailed into harbour a lone piper welcomed us home. We were to be in camp at Basingstoke. It was the greatest feeling to be on English soil once again, and finally, embarkation leave.

On meeting up with my family, I was to find my father was in good health; however my mother's health had deteriorated. She was diabetic. My brother Eric was in hospital having another operation on his leg. He had Osteomyelitis. He was three years younger than I. My youngest brother Dennis was still an evacuee, continuing to reside in Sussex with his host family on their small holding.

On leave at the same time and living nearby were several commandos and men from other units. We were to join up later. My particular pal at this time was Ray Craddock from 2 Commando who I had met up with in Italy.

It was party time. Harry Cherry from 4 Commando, Ray Craddock and I were sitting in a pub. We'd been through the "welcome home" bit and were now wondering what to do with our time. "Let's have a party" said Harry. "No girls," said a moody Ray. "You can't have a party without girls! How many girls do you know?" He challenged. We reflected we'd been out of touch with the local talent far too long.

We sat pensively looking into our beer. "Woolworths," I said. "That could be the answer." Woolworths was a well-known name to anybody who shopped, one on every high street in town and famous (in those days) for its slogan, "Nothing over sixpence" It stocked all the smaller necessities of life such as combs, razors blades, and haberdashery and so on. Our local Woolworths, one of the larger stores at the Broadway in Tooting, had a series of counters, each with one or two young females serving the customers.

"What about Woolworths?" asked Ray. "There must be girls there who would like to go to a party." I said. My mind started ticking over. "Look, we could go round with a clip board type of thing. We go up to each of the girls and we say something like, 'Excuse me dear, are you married?' if they say yes then we thank them and move on. We go to the next one and ask the same question. If they say 'No' we then ask if they are engaged. If they say 'yes' we thank them and move on. We ask the next one the same thing. When we find a girl who is not married or engaged we then invite them to our party. We write down on a slip of paper where the party is and at what time." We decided to put the plan into action. We agreed to hold the first party at my parents' home with my parents to stay with my mother's sister during the evening.

Harry and I nominated ourselves as the "interviewers". It was a roaring success! As we went from one counter to another the word got around about the party before we got to the next counter and so we were greeted with a smiling face and "Can I come?" Wearing uniforms and green berets seemed to have done the trick.

Soaked in success we reported to the pub and informed Ray. It slowly dawned on us; maybe we had over reached ourselves! Now we had more women than we had men. In those days telephones were virtually non-existent. Desperately we thought of others on leave and of cousins and the like to make up the shortage. With a bit of a struggle we managed to overcome the shortfall of men, particularly by others on leave.

The next problem was the supply of drink and things to eat. The latter was overcome by assistance from parents. Everything was in short supply. But with the help of an obliging young mother who loaned us the baby's pram we went from one source to another and succeeded in obtaining the essential supplies of alcohol.

With objects that took up space or would be easily broken removed from the main two rooms we were about ready. We had a stroke of luck on the music front. It turned out Ray's father was a violinist who knew a pianist who, provided he was kept in booze, would play all night. Turned out he was terrific. An Irishmen of around fifty with a red face and an attractive hoarse voice he was the life and soul of the party, thumping out song after song on our Barnes piano. Some initially shy, the girls soon got into the mood of the evening. Many partnered up and with Mike bellowing at the top of his voice and his fingers dancing over the keys it turned into a great night.

The success of the party had put down a marker that we were home and we were available. A Woolworth's visit at any time after was greeted with welcoming smiles and waves from girls who had spread the word.

We followed this up with similar do's at Ray's place shortly afterwards. We had found drinking glasses to be in short supply. We overcame this by drinking out of jam jars. It was during this period I was to meet a girl who later became a big part of my life, my future wife, Barbara Dean a slim, rather shy nineteen year old with grey eyes and thick auburn hair.

With disembarkation leave over I returned to Basingstoke and started re-training. It was widely expected our next move would be to the Far East.

The war in Europe came to an end. At sometime a victory parade took place in London. An atom bomb was dropped on Hiroshima to be followed shortly afterwards by another on Nagasaki. Japan Surrendered.

Finally we were at peace. Apart from all the momentous action following from this, the top brass were at a loss as what to do with us. When they made up their minds we were posted to Germany.

At Recklinghausen a temporary lager of high wire fencing had been erected to hold Nazi Germans. It became the task of 2 Commando to guard the prisoners. Life was relaxed with plenty of off duty time. Men were now waiting for the day they were to return to civilian life.

Near by was the small town of Herne. One evening a couple of friends and I visited a 'Bierstube', a pub. I had picked up a number of words of German as had my friends, who ordered light beers. I preferred a slightly sweeter drink and so specified "Eine Dunkel" beer, which is more akin to a stout. (my favourite English drink in those days was a 'brown & mild').

As we moved through the patrons to get to our table we passed three young women seated on a long stool. "Sind sie mit kind, Herr Grune Mutze?" meaning 'are you pregnant, Mr. Green Beret?" I stopped, surprised. The woman in the middle of the three was looking at me gravely. The others giggled. She pointed to the glass in my hand. "Dunkel Bier" she said. I then understood what she was saying. Dark brown beer was taken by pregnant women as an aid to child birth.

"Not yet," I replied, with a smile, and moved on. Every time I looked in their direction I caught the eye of the middle woman and her smile.

A couple of nights later I was back at the pub. She was

seated at a table. I joined her. Her name was Lieselotte. She spoke few words of English. I was immediately attracted to her. About 5'3" her dark wavy brown hair framed an attractive face. She was in her twenties, several years older than me, with a cheeky sense of humour. I was aware that things were desperate in Germany at the end of the war and a number of liaisons were made in the desire for food and goods. I was also at that time, cynical about the German nation and its population. Places and deeds such as 'Belsen', did not endear me to them.

Nevertheless, our relationship grew. I was introduced to her family. The mother was a typical German frau whose interest in life was maternal, attempting to achieve the basics of life for her family, such as food, health, hygiene, as Germany, at the time was a starving nation in critical need of food and basic supplies. Her father was a slightly built man with a quiet way of speaking, very courteous and charming.

My caution gradually faded as we got to know each other. We went to an opera house and a type of music hall, to a pub where we were not known. Thing developed. It became quite passionate. Most of my spare time was spent in her company. The family had in addition to their own home a second property on a nearby garden estate which we occupied. It became obvious that her feelings for me were quite genuine and let's face it; I felt the same about her. I had never known anybody like her. She had a great sense of humour, very sensitive, very attractive and with a small pert nose and deep searching eyes, very attractive. My German improved pretty rapidly

. As I got to know the family I found that her father had long been in an opposition party to the Nazi party and had been imprisoned as a result of his anti-Nazi views. Initially with my hard attitude to all things German I took this with a large pinch of salt however eventually believing it to be true.. Slowly I noticed the great respect shown by other Germans towards him and their greetings when meeting him on the street. He was not a well man and some time later I was to hear he had died.

Things were rather lax at our unit in Recklinghausen. After any duties I would catch the transport into Herne and spend my time with Liesel. The following morning I would return to camp on the tram.

It was a happy, passionate time for both of us. However, the action determined by the War Office was to come as a shock. The whole of the army Commandos were to be disbanded. Men were to return to their original units where they were, which was mostly the United Kingdom. It had been long known that the Commando ethic was not one approved or liked by certain top brass. With the war ended there was no further requirement for their use. The Royal Marines with their specialised personnel would carry on. Volunteers were no longer required. With others I discussed the situation. Many were due for demobilising shortly so were not too bothered. My own demob date had been fixed for later in the following year 1946. I still had a few months to do. I desperately wanted to stay in Germany until any inevitable return to civilian life.

I found the answer. Germany had been divided into four sectors: British, Russian, American and French. With Germany in the shattered state it was, each had a Commission dealing with the problems of the sectors. Initially there had been a non-fraternisation policy with the Germans. This in the British section had been eased over a period but problems still remained.

I made an application to join the British "Control Commission of Germany" (C.C.G), jovially referred to as "Charlie Chaplin's Grenadiers." The Commission although civilian, had a military element within it, carrying out security duties. My application was accepted much to the joy of Liesel. But we were to find it had a snag.

I was now a part of the Control Commission. I was to keep my uniform and green beret until I became a civilian. I was to be posted to Kiel in Slesgwig Holstein near the Danish border. I was presently further south in the Ruhrgebeit district not too far from Cologne. It was quite a distance and an obstacle in our relationship, however, Liesel vowed to follow me anywhere. Tearfully, she hung tightly to me on my departure and said she loved me 'ich liebe dich', she whispered. "du bist mein zigeuner". Her gypsy and I suppose, with my black hair, brown eyes and tanned skin I looked the type! Then I was gone with promises to write.

Kiel was a large port and housed the local branch of the Control Commission. I didn't care for the place over much and was therefore delighted to be posted to the town of Neumunster where a detachment operated.

This turned out to be occupying a large rambling German house of several floors and a German staff of a waitress, cook, assistant and cleaners.

The civilian staff of a few British civil servants occupied offices on the ground floor and seemed to work 9 to 5 when they would disappear to their own accommodation. The military element of some half a dozen soldiers from a mixture of units lived on the higher floors each had his own room.

With a large dining room, waitress service and good food from the kitchen we were well looked after. The duties were certainly not arduous. It would appear my particular tasks were to take care of the guns and knives that the German civilians had been instructed to hand in. A heavy wooden door with an aperture cut into it gave access to a cellar which would house these items. By the time I arrived at Neumunster the bulk of the 'donations' had already been handed in, creating a large pile of guns and sharp edged weapons in the cellar. My job was to box this lot. A steady stream of weapons passed through that door.

Another of the duties I was to perform was to be responsible for the accommodation we provided for travellers. Above our accommodation a large attic spread from one end of the building to the other. With eighteen beds it could accommodate groups of entertainers and the like who passed through the town. On a number of occasions dance troops from neighbouring countries, Romania, Hungary and others were so accommodated. Young good looking females occupying beds above the heads of half a dozen virile soldiers ready and willing seemed to be too much for many of the ladies who made themselves available in all senses of the word.

Compared to the others I led a more monastic life, which incidentally seemed to be resented by one of the men. This man from one of the corps was unpleasant. Apart from his drinking and insulting the staff, particularly Hedda, our waitress, he tried to throw his weight about in a number of ways. He had a weird sense of humour such as putting salt in an unsuspecting soldier's tea. From what I gathered he had been the first soldier to arrive at Neumunster which in his eyes seemed to make him the senior member.

I had been at the detachment only a few days when an incident occurred. We were seated at the long table where dinner was being served. Opposite me sat this guy, smoking a cigarette. Hedda had just served several of us. I had turned round to speak to Hedda. Turning back to my meal and about to pick up cutlery I stopped dead. Protruding from the food on my plate was a stubbed out cigarette. Looking up I saw a grinning oaf opposite. Table conversation died away. I was angry, bloody angry. The cheek of the man! I stood up. Lifted my steaming plate of food on one hand and slung it at the face before me. Seeing what I was about to do, he managed to duck and the cracked plate and mess of food slid slowly down the wall behind him. I sat down, leaned towards him, and said quietly, "you ever do a thing like that again, I'll kill you!" I was never troubled again and the salt in the tea of others also became a thing of the past. Eventually his demob number came up and he departed.

Later a much happier occasion arose. Liesel had taken the "D' zug" – The fast train to Neumunster and there she was smiling and waving at me at the station. It was a longish journey and I was impressed as well as delighted, I arranged a room next to mine and unofficially took some time off. We were so aware time was running out. My demobilisation date was rapidly arriving. Every moment was precious, but finally, inevitably it was to arrive.

The day before, I was to put Liesel on a train returning her to Herne. Liesel was in tears and I was feeling choked. With one last tight embrace and smothering me with kisses, she boarded the train and was gone.

I have mentioned, briefly, Hedda our waitress. Now I have given considerable thought to whether I should put down the following, or leave it and move to other matters. There are a number of reasons for this. Not least it puts me in a pretty poor light. Some may think I've dreamt it up. On that point I assure you that is not so.

I may have mentioned that Hedda was around twenty two or so. It appeared that she was unusually fortunate in that the war in some senses had not impacted upon her as I had seen elsewhere. She was from a somewhat isolated farming family which may have had a lot to do with it. How or why she had taken the job of waitress in the small town of Neumunster escaped me.

However, the job wasn't at all arduous and with her blonde hair, pleasant features and good manners, other than the oaf I have already mentioned, she was treated by the half a dozen soldiers with respect. Her shyness was often reflected in her nervousness when the soldiers joked with her in broken German. It became obvious to me that she had had a pretty sheltered life with limited companionships.

There was a certain amount of coming and going with the fellows and the various females of the dancing troupes. My own love life was or had been taken care of so you could say I didn't need to indulge.

I had noticed that Hedda had taken some sort of a shine to me. She seemed to be more at ease in my presence and during quiet periods when most of my compatriots were in town or in their rooms she would bring me a cup of tea or I'd invite her to sit and we'd have a chat to improve my German.

It was during these conversations I noticed a nervous or shyness in her. As she stood sometimes at the door about to depart, she would look at me and her face would flush crimson and she would leave quickly

On one occasion she was sitting quietly, then she spoke quickly in German. I looked up astonished. I had obviously misunderstood what she was asking me. She said it again. Her face aflame. She was asking if I would sleep with her. Please. Bitte.

I took her hand and tried to reduce her nervousness. She said she was not joking. I said I was most honoured to be asked. But why? She was a beautiful young lady, so why?

It flooded out. She had never been with a man. She knew she was shy. She felt it to be the right time. I was a "good" man. Unlike the others who shouted of their conquests to each other. She felt I was different.

I was in a most unusual situation. I looked at her, at the tears that were about to drop. I decided. I stood up. Wrapped her in my arms and said simply "Ok. You decide when and where."

For the first (and only) time in my life I had been- what can I say- propositioned?

Later, as arranged, she came to my room. She was shaking with nervousness. I said, "Drink this" and gave her a glass of whisky. She didn't like it. I poured in water to weaken it. I put my arms around her. "Hedda", I said softly "are you sure you want to?" Slowly her shaking subsided and she breathed "Yes."

The following day I avoided breakfast. At lunch our eyes met and I was greated with a brilliant smile. She seemed much happier. Not long afterwards my time with the Control Commission of Germany came to an end

For all these years I have kept my promise to Hedda to tell no one.

Now it doesn't seem to matter, you are the first to be told.

PHOTOS: WORLD WAR II

Tunisia – Stretcher Bearers of the East Surrey Regiment, during the attack on Longstop Hill on 23 April 1943.

Italy – Lt. John Woodhouse leads members of the Surreys' Battle Patrol.

Italy - The Battle Patrol resting. 1943. From left to right: Reg Cambridge, John Varney, Lt. John 'Charlie' Woodhouse, Eric Monsey, Dennis Scaife.

Left: Italy – December 1943. Battle Patrol colleague, Pte. Robinson, armed with his Thompson SMG, grenades and knife.

Right: Lt. John Woodhouse, Dorset Regiment. Battle Patrol Commanding Officer.

Left: Dennis 'Lou' Scaife. 1943. Note the 78th Division badge, a golden battle-axe was worn above the left breast pocket by members of the Surreys' Battle Patrol.

CERTIFIED TRUE COPY.

From: Lieut. J.M.Woodhouse, M.C., O.C.Battle Patrol, 1/East
Surrey Regt.
SUBJECT: Private R.G.Cambridge.

With a view that the abilities of the above soldier
at present under my command be used to the best advantage
in the event of the disbandment of the Battle Patrol. I
set down here my considered opinion of his military values.

He volunteered to serve in the Battle Patrol when it
reformed after almost complete annihilation on the 15th
October, 1943.

Since that time he has carried out between 20 and 25
patrols nearly all of them under my command. He has shown
on every occasion that we have been in close contact with
enemy troops complete self control and displayed always a skill
in night movement even higher than the very high standard
maintained in the Battle Patrol.

He has been recommended for a decoration for his
determination when amongst an enemy tank harbour on the SANGRO
River 13/14th November last year.

That Private Cambridge does not rank any higher is because
of his persistent refusal to accept promotion. If he has been
in any case obliged to leave the Battle Patrol I hope that
he will accept the responsibility that his ability demands
and hope that you may be able to persuade him to do this.

Private Cambridge is a born leader who needs only the
training in order to command a platoon or Company. In my
considered opinion he should be pushed as far as possible.
In the present desperate shortage of all junior leaders he
can be absolutely invaluable.

I hope you will get great value from this young soldier
and confidently believe you will as I have for the past six
months.

1st March, 1944.

(Signed) D.M.WOODHOUSE. Lieut.

Testimonial for Reg Cambridge, written by Lt. John Woodhouse following the disbanding of the Battle Patrol and most definitely the reason for my successful attempt at joining the Commandos.

130

Eric Monsey was killed in action in Italy at the age of 20 years after the disbanding of the Battle Patrol. He is buried in the Military Cemetery at Agenta Gap, Italy. He was a great pal and fellow soldier. He is missed greatly and remembered fondly.

CHAPTER 12
CIVVY STREET, NOT PAVED WITH GOLD

My time was up. The army (and Charlie Chaplin's Grenadiers), no longer required my services! I returned to England, handed in all military kit and in return was given a civilian suit, a raincoat a few other items of clothing, and a trilby hat.

My AB64 Pt II was handed back to me with dates of enlistment and discharge. An assessment of my military conduct was entered as 'good', which was one step above 'poor' and below 'very good' and 'exemplary'.

As I caught the train home I felt mixed emotions. Things would never be the same again, I thought. I was filled with the pleasure of seeing my family. I remember feeling self-conscious of wearing a suit and a raincoat over my arm. Behind me was a life in which I had made a small niche in which I had fitted, and before me? I hadn't a clue. I consoled myself by the fact many thousands were in the same boat and facing the same situation. But right now I had embarkation leave money in my pocket, the war was over and I had survived. That was enough to raise my spirits. The future could look after itself!

Following the inevitable rounds of re-unions with relatives, meeting up with friends who had survived the war, I settled down to civilian life. Well, I tried to settle down. It all seemed very strange. Dennis Scaife returned home from being a prisoner of war, which was the excuse for another party. Barbara (or Babs) became a regular part of my life. Very popular with my family, I used to meet her on a daily basis and we'd have lunch together usually at the ABC restaurant at the Broadway. She worked at a local firm which produced temperature gauges. Each evening we'd be in each other's company, and meeting up with friends we'd go dancing at the Strand ballroom, Wimbledon dance Hall, Streatham ice rink and several other local dives. I particularly liked going to the Strand. At one time it had been a theatre- it had a slightly sloping floor and a balcony overlooking the dancers. It ran dances from late evening to around 5 o'clock the following morning. Our little gang would then seek out the Lyons Corner House restaurant nearby and have breakfast before we made our way back to the Broadway.

Writing of dancing and dance halls reminds me of earlier times. I suppose I was sixteen when I with couple of mates thought it a good idea to learn to dance and so enrolled in Nina Mason's School of Dancing which was located in Balham. After standing on our partner's toes over several weeks we learnt the basic steps of quick-step and fox-trot and although we were rubbish at dancing we would try practising steps all the way back to Tooting Broadway.
 All brilliantined and wearing our best (and only!) suit, we would sally forth on Saturday nights to dances at places like Wimbledon Palais and Wimbledon Town Hall and spend a perspiring evening treading on more female toes.
 I can remember Oscar Rabin and his orchestra playing at the Palais and the Resident Band at Wimbledon Town Hall, whose name I will never forget was 'Arthur Forrest and His Trans - Atlantic Killer Dillers.'
 Can there be anyone else still existing who remembers that band?

I needed to find a job and earn some money. So I visited the local employment exchange. There were signs the world was inevitably changing. One small thing has always stuck in my mind. Prewar an applicant for work would address the employment clerk (always men) as "Sir" and the clerk expected such. I know this was so as I had accompanied my father on several occasions in the past. This was no longer happening. Returning soldiers and others who used the exchanges were in no mood for such. So I sat in the employment exchange and finally ended up at the counter. "What can you do?" enquired the man behind the counter. I thought for a moment. I had no desire to return to engineering. Well I don't really have a particular trade" I replied. The clerk's brow furrowed as he flicked through a number of cards. He stopped at one. "Ah," he said, reading the card. "Without a trade it's difficult to find anything." He looked up "But," he tapped the card, "the council is looking for a grave digger..."he stopped. He must have seen the look on my face. "It's all I can offer at the moment." Back home I told my family of the offer. They thought it funny. I felt a bit insulted! Later, through meeting an ex-serviceman in a pub, I got myself fixed up with a steady little job with an outfit supplying local schools with books, teaching materials, and so on. It was run from a disused school building in Mitcham. It didn't pay much but I thought it would do till I sorted out my future. The job was a doddle. Each morning several vans would draw up at our place of work. The previous day we had prepared the supplies pre-ordered. Having loaded the vans which then went off on their various journeys we had pretty well finished for the day. After a tidying up and prep-orders for the following day our work was done. Half a dozen of us, all ex-service chaps, shared the tasks between us and then settled down in front of a fire (if a cold day) smoked and chatted. Being all in the service until a few months previously the subject of our conversation was based around military life.

Outlandish anecdotes and personal over-imaginative exploits resulted in a listener standing up and gave a suspended electric light fitting a shove. This was referred to as "swinging the lamp' and expressed the opinion that the listeners were being regaled with a load of bull-shit. After a while I realised the job was making me lazy and also it held no future. I was becoming irritable and found civilian life boring. Another attraction- although I used it more as an excuse really – was the army offering a small incentive to ex-service men to re-join their regiment on a 3 year engagement with a financial offer of 25 pounds down and 25 pounds per year. Of course this didn't sit well with Barbara who didn't look forward to being separated. But I pointed out that the East Surreys depot was at Kingston-on-Thames, only a stones throw from where we lived. I made some enquiries, confirmed I would be put on the strength of the depot staff, and took the plunge. I signed on for three years.

In many ways I questioned whether I had done the right thing in re-joining the army, for I realised quite soon that my love/hate attitude to the regiment still existed and that chip on my shoulder was still there and would be getting bigger. But my choice was limited. The army Commandos had been disbanded and were no more and to get the financial bonus I had to join an outfit I had been serving with.
My first realisation that the invisible chip was still sitting on my shoulder was on my first parade, before I had been allocated a staff job. The depot at that time was taking and training (I believe) men called up for national service. Newly kitted out in uniform, smartly pressed in all the appropriate areas, boots highly polished and wearing medal ribbons I stood on parade as the RSM with his usual contingent of company Sgt Major, Duty-Sgt and so on

trailing along behind him walked along the men facing directly to their front, inspecting each man as he passed, ramrod straight and pacing stick under his right arm exactly horizontal to the ground. I was in the front row. With measured step he was about to pass me when he stopped, turned back and said "Don't I know you? It's Cambridge, isn't it?" "Yes, Sir" I replied.

Now RSM Wooley of the Guards Regiment had been posted as RSM to the 1st Bn East Surreys during its campaigns in North Africa and Italy. I had come to his attention on several occasions such as the incident of the Sicilian 'holiday'. So he inspected my turnout, couldn't fault it, and said with a sneer. "Couldn't make it in civilian life, eh?" "Well Sir," I replied. "I found there are just as many bastards in civvy street as there are in the army, Sir." He gazed silently at me for a moment. Then turning to the CSM said "Put this soldier on the staff of the Regimental Police." He then continued his inspection of the parade.

I was home, back in the army, back in what I knew. Back into this odd masochistic bitter sweet relationship, however, a relationship I understood.

CHAPTER 13
POACHER TURNED GAMEKEEPER

So a Regimental Policeman (R.P) I became. It was an easy going job. Smart turnout was of course the essence. It was more of a day time occupation which meant one was not liable for guard duties at night. Each evening a seven man guard parade took place outside the guard room. The Duty Officer would decide the smartest turnout. The selected soldier would thus avoid the two hours on guard and four hours off that the remaining six would be required to carry out and get a nights sleep. If I recall rightly, the "stickman" as the smartest turned out soldier was called, would become the following day's Company Commander duty runner – an easy number.

The daily routine of guard room life for an R.P. followed a pattern. The morning routine of Regimental Police enabled the Guard Commander and his men to hand back their guard room – in clean condition. Prisoners and cells would be inspected and checked. The guard report completed and signed and off would go the soldiers. The Provost Sgt and his R.P.s back in control and preparing to take a couple of prisoners to the cook house and collect breakfast for prisoners and staff. I had bed space allocated to me in the permanent staff barrack room. I rarely slept there.

My parent's home in Tooting or Upper Tooting as some residents referred to the area which led up to Tooting Bec Common – was only a few miles from the Kingston – on – Thames barracks. Each morning I would leave home and cycle to the barrack gates where I'd dismount, stow the bike and put on my prepared pressed battle dress and polished boots. Should I be delayed or otherwise make a non-appearance my friends on the R.Ps would cover for me. When the day's work was done, back on my bike and back to Tooting, family and girlfriend. Life was pleasant except for one thing. I had a running complaint with the military authorities over my pay.

I had only been out of the army a few months but on re-enlistment I had been put on the lowest rate of an infantry soldier. The only way I could increase my pay rate was to undergo a series of infantry tests – that would result in becoming what was known as a 5 star infantry man. The big problem was when was I going to get tested. It was several months before I could get on the courses and the chip on my shoulder just became larger!

So the months passed. But army life has an unerring way of providing unanticipated surprises. This one came out of the blue and gave me a certain amount of grief as I will explain.

The layout of military guard rooms are pretty much the same. Positioned just inside the main gate the building comprises a large guard room. Often with red or brown painted floor and a centrally located strip of red carpet from entrance to the main desk. At the rear of the desk a passage to the toilet and cells.

At the particular time I'm about to relate we had a couple of delinquents in the cells with short sentences to complete and causing us no particular trouble.

One day a police car drew up and a well dressed civilian was escorted into the guard room. This was our first introduction to Harry Green (as I shall call him), a slightly tubby figure, a round rather podgy face which gave the impression he had fed well. His suit was of excellent cut and he had a prosperous look about him.

We were informed Mr. Green was a long time deserter from the armed forces and as we were the most convenient and nearest military guard room it had been agreed he was to be held until such time his original unit collected him.

Harry Green was an interesting man,. He had 'done a runner' just after his military call-up and built up a profitable business in making and providing beauty products to a grateful female population. It was the first time during the period I had been on R.P. that we had a civilian clothed person in the cells. He had a polite friendly manner and seemed to accept his future with good grace.

After a few days we got used to him. He kept his cell tidy and with a Regimental Police in attendance swept the passages and volunteered to do a number of other small duties. Said he liked to be occupied. He got on particularly well with the R.P Corporal who virtually ran the show in the absence of the Provost Sergeant.

To be honest we didn't see a lot of the Provost Sgt. He certainly had other duties that took place beyond the guard room and had a liking for the bar of the Sergeant's Mess.

Each meal time a small group consisting of prisoners and escorts would go to the Mess Hall and collect the food for all in the guard room.

One particular day I was just returning to the guard room from dealing with specific tasks two men on 'Jankers' (defaulter's) were to carry out at the Sergeants Mess kitchen, when the Corporal and an R.P. plus two prisoners were about to leave the guard room to collect the evening meal. It was the beginning of November and was quite dark although only about four o'clock.

I was writing up the defaulters book when I said to Peter Davenport one of the R.P. to check out the prisoner Harry Green. Other than Green we only had two prisoners at the time and they were getting the evening meal. Peter dropped what he was doing and sauntered into the cell block. He came back with a confused look on his face. "Green is not in his cell which is unlocked. Did he go to get the meal with the Corporal?" "Check the toilets!

Quick!" I commanded with a nasty feeling trouble was a brewing. Peter came back shaking his head his face white. "Not there." By this time I was on my feet and in the cell block. The cell door was unlocked but pushed close. I checked the cell window bars. Unlike those in Gravesend all those years ago these were firmly in position. A check of every part of the building confirmed what I now knew. That Green had done another runner. How, I had no idea. It was confirmed later he had not gone through the main gate, where an R.P. had been on duty. In the darkness and wearing dark civilian clothes once outside the perimeters he would vanish.

The report of a loss of a prisoner caused no end of panic and trouble. Later, when I thought about it it had seemed unusual to say the least, for the Corporal to escort prisoners to collect meals. I couldn't remember him doing so before.

With the prisoner gone it now became, whose head was to be served on a plate. The Corporal swore he checked the cells before he left the Guard room. It couldn't have been more than five minutes from me returning from the defaulter job and a check of the cells. As the senior man on the premises when the loss of the prisoner was discovered and the fact that the military had to find someone to blame, it became obvious who was to take the blame. Me! How Harry Green disappeared was a mystery but slowly I realised he would have needed help. With the coming and goings of prisoners and escorts and minor jobs being done covering could only be provided by a member of the guard room personnel.

So a quick inquiry was held. As senior person at the Guardroom at the time the prisoner's escape was discovered I was held responsible and charged with negligence. Loss of a person in close confinement was a court-martial offence. After being on 'open' arrest for several weeks I was marched before a board of three senior officers and charged with "Without reasonable excuse allowing to escape a person when it was his duty to guard". Tried by District Courts-Martial at Kingston-on-Thames on 4 December 1947 and found "guilty".

I had pleaded not guilty and put up a spirited defence with a good defending officer but knowing how the military works, knew what the outcome would be. But some of the defence argument must have been considered for I was sentenced to undergo Detention for 168 Hours! Which of course is 7 days. A loss of pay would have been normal for a detention sentence. In this case the 7 days loss of pay was later cancelled.

I was incarcerated in my own Guardroom and so chose my favourite cell. My brother Eric visited with a number of books and packs of cigarettes and I settled down to a pleasant week. I had requested "leave to appeal" which was a nice phrase I'd picked up from the Army Manual on being found guilty, which had made a bit of a furore at the District Courts- Martial, but I didn't bother to proceed with it. It was decided at my request that I should no longer carry on as a Regimental Policeman. And once again on a change of direction I landed on my feet.

I was made ration clerk. What a wonderful job! Other than a Lance-corporal who was to become a great friend we were left to carry out our job of providing and collecting the units rations from a warehouse depot and distributing according to numbers of personnel, to the Officers, Sergeants and other ranks Messes.

Left entirely to ourselves it was a cracking good job. David the Lance-corporal had been doing the job for quite a while and had it down to a 'T'.

Once a week the Company Sgt-Majors who lived with their families on or nearby the barracks were provided with a weekend joint which had been 'scrounged' with other items from the staff at the food depot. This ensured we were never required for any other military duty. Figures could always be inflated if necessary. Figures for personnel on leave could always be overlooked. My favourite late breakfast meal was always a pleasure. A large china mug of cornflakes topped by evaporated milk, a hand full of peanuts and sultanas sweetened from a large sack of sugar in which a pencil had penetrated making a neat small hole.

Between us we had plenty of time on our hands and often arranged it so one could have a day off. I can still remember David calling at my house with a chicken he had 'picked up' for me when I was on leave. We had a great time - everybody was so friendly…

It was during this time I saw a notice on the company notice board from the Intelligence Corps asking for suitable personnel. Now, in truth I had never heard of the Intelligence Corps. I was intrigued and dashed off an application.

Subsequently I received instruction to attend an interview in London. I was on leave at the time and the request carried no little excitement and cheeky remarks at home. The notice had said a knowledge of foreign languages would be an advantage and in the appropriate place I had entered 'some knowledge of German and Italian'.

I will never forget that interview. It took place in one of the government buildings in central London.

When I entered the waiting room I was to find a Warrant Officer, a Sergeant and a Corporal waiting to be interviewed. As a private I was certainly out ranked and beginning to think I was wasting my time.

In true military form each was to be called in rank order. In went the Sgt-major. Whilst we had been waiting I had got on well with the Sgt who was from the Rifle Brigade, the only other infantry man. We decided we would let each other know how we got on.

After half an hour or so the W.O. reappeared, gave us the thumbs down and said 'Tough interview' and was gone. My new friend the Sgt. was called in.

When he returned to the waiting room he was all smiles. He had passed, he said. The Corporal now went in. when he returned he gave the thumbs down sign. The Sergeant said he would wait to see what my outcome would be.

I went in a large room with large windows. In the window alcove a civilian lounged with his hands in his pockets.

Seated at a baize covered table were three men in civilian clothes. The central man was older than the other two, with grey hair looking quite distinguished.

In the centre of the room was a wooden chair, where I was indicated to sit.

The grey haired man opened the proceedings, with a series of routine questions. My name, age, unit and so on. Then another man asked a series of questions. Why did I wish to join the Intelligence Corps, where did I go to school, give a summary of my military service, then other inquiries concerning my background and family details.

The third man then chimed in stating the type of person they were looking for would then attend a detailed course in military intelligence when it would be decided if the applicant was the right material for a career in the Corps. It was then the guy in the window seat interrupted. In German he asked me a number of questions. Where I had lived in Germany and so on. How had I learned German. This was a bit tricky but I explained I had a long term German girlfriend and conversed within the German family. He asked a few more questions I managed to answer.

He then switched to Italian. He certainly was a linguist. I answered his questions as best as I could.

In English he said.

"Your understanding of the languages is adequate. But your grammar is bloody awful." I then turned back to the men at the board table who continued to question me.

One of the younger men said "Well, Cambridge, we are unsure whether you may be suitable. Have you anything you would like to say?"

"Sir," I replied, "With the right training I believe I would be an asset to the Intelligence Corps. All I ask is that I be allowed to attend the course to be able to prove this to you."

To which the grey headed man said. "You appear to be an intelligent man and I have no doubt you will do well. So we will accept your application and will confirm the date of transfer in due course."

The Rifle Brigade Sgt was waiting to hear the outcome of my interview "I'm in!" I said gleefully and we went off to a café, where we discussed our futures.

It was the last time I saw my new found friend. Perhaps his regiment prevailed upon him to remain with them. The pull of a regiment can be quite strong, but I looked forward to this new opening and I was to find I had finally found my slot in the scheme of things.

CHAPTER 14
MARRIAGE & THE INTELLIGENCE CORPS

It will be appreciated that an Intelligence organisation places restriction on the divulging of its activities. I left the Intelligence Corps, over 40 years ago but much of its activities continues in the same pattern albeit in a more modern fashion. As a qualified Interrogator and Counter Intelligence operator I was involved in certain situations which were of interest to me and the Intelligence Corps, but remain in the past. With almost twenty years in the Corps I therefore write of incidents which remain in my memory but were more or less incidental to my main activities.

At that time the Intelligence Corps HQ was based at Maresfield in Sussex; located in a small estate of Countryside shielded by a large stand of trees. It had its own private roads on which I was later to train to ride a motorcycle.

Some twenty or so men attended the course. It lasted several weeks and without boasting I can say I did very well. For me the subjects were interesting, the instructors knew their business and I knew my army life was heading in a completely new dimension. I felt I was now doing something worthwhile.

I had been Positively Vetted (PV) and later obtained higher classified access to certain locations and information.

My posting overseas came through, with notice of my immediate embarkation leave. At home my news was met with mixed feelings. Singapore was to be my next destination and would probably be a couple of years before it coincided with the end of the three year service I had signed on for. My family thought it would be an exciting posting. But when I told Barbara the news she didn't see it in quite the same way.

The first part of my embarkation leave was taken up with visits to relatives and having fun. Barbara's brother Alan, a former medic in the Royal Navy was about to marry and as such provided a certain amount of fuss in her mother's household.

Alan's marriage duly took place with of course many guests and family and in the light of the food and other shortages existing at that time it was quite "a do".

A short time after the wedding Babs and I were discussing my overseas posting. I was very happy with my transfer to a specialist part of the armed forces. Babs said she was pleased for me but then dissolved into tears, as she spoke of my imminent departure and the many months – even years – I would be gone. It wasn't the best marriage proposal ever uttered, but I said, "Well, we could get married. Maybe I could get married accommodation out there." There was little doubt we loved each other. "Can we marry? Have we the time to get married before you go?" She asked. I checked the dates. It looked doubtful. Alan had spent ages organising his wedding. I had just over a week before I returned to my unit. In my infantry days I would have probably taken some extra days of absence. This mind set no longer applied.

"If you really want to marry, I don't know much about the pros and cons. But we haven't the time to arrange a church wedding. Although to be honest that wouldn't bother me. Maybe we can get married in a Registrar's Office. But that would mean you would miss out on every girls dream of a white wedding and all the trimmings." I said. "I wouldn't care about any of that." She said, tearfully. "I just want to marry you." I kissed her tears away and said, "ok. I will see what I can do in the short time we have."

Making enquiries I found that although notice was short providing we were both free of encumbrances, such as former spouse, I could arrange to get married at Wandsworth Town Hall in a few days time. I confirmed this would take place and gave a happy Babs the news.

My parents were delighted. Babs was very popular with all my family. It was slightly different with her people. Her mother had just seen her eldest son married off and had incurred some expenditure and effort. Our immediate intentions rather caught them off balance.

The wedding took place as planned. Babs looked terrific in her pink two piece. In 1948 the only photographs were in black and white and I have them on the wall still. I looked respectable in uniform.

My mother's sister, my favourite Aunt Em, took care of the food and drinks and the event went off quite well.

Aunt Em and Uncle Will owned a furnished property in Tonsley Hill, Wandsworth, the former home of Uncle Will's now deceased parents. They had previously offered it to me for free. A lovely cottage, which had I been a civilian I would have been delighted to own. But it had war damage to the rear wall and I was not then in a position to take it on.

But it was ideal for Babs and I to spend our first days together. We married on the third of August 1948. The previous month I had my 25th birthday. Babs had been twenty two on the 10th of June the month prior to mine. So now we were a grown up married couple.

A few days later I had to return to Maresfield to prepare for my embarkation. I believe we married on the Tuesday and I departed on the Friday leaving a tearful Babs at the station.

Having been kitted up and arms swollen with inoculations we sailed on, I believe the "Empire Halladale". The first time I had been on a ship in peace time. How different. No overcrowding and no anticipation and fear of a torpedo coming our way. With several Corps personnel aboard for company it was a pleasant and interesting voyage.

Disembarking at Singapore we were at first billeted at Nee Soon Transit-Camp. Here we were to experience the monsoon weather. Deep open concrete channels took the flood waters out to sea. I recall an incident that took place when the young child of a permanent staff Warrant Officer fell into the open drains and was swept away by the swirling water. By good fortune a grille on this particular channel halted her progress and soldiers managed to save her and return her to her distraught parents.

I was in Singapore at what was called Singapore Special Intelligence Section for a short time only. Among other duties I recall it dealt with port security. It was here I was to find my eventual posting was to be to 355 Field Security Section which had its headquarters in Kuala Lumpur the capital of Malaya, with detachments at Johore Baru (J.B.), Seremban, Kluang, Muar and Port Dickson.

Further north of Kuala Lumpur (K.L.) the only other Intelligence Section in that part of the world was 358 F.S. Section. When I joined 355 F.S.S the Field Security Officer (FSO) in charge of the Section was a Capt. John McPhail, who later was replaced by Captain 'Les' Masterson. Originally the Company Sgt-Major of 355 was a Liverpudlian Les Jones later to be replaced by C.S.M Jack Swaney. The reason British troops were in Malaya among others was to combat the Communist Terrorists (C.T.) as they were called. It will be remembered in 1948 and for a couple of years longer Malaya although virtually remaining it own country, was a British Colony. When Japan invaded Malaya and Singapore the British had a disastrous campaign with Japanese victories. The British returned after the Japanese surrender in 1945, but now the countries were demanding Merdeka! Freedom from foreign rule. In the fifties Malaya and Singapore were to get their individual Merdeka, but this period of 1948-1950 was to be my first and only experience of 'Colonial Rule,' albeit much watered down.

It was, after my previous infantry service quite a wonderful period of my life. I loved it! I was with a great bunch of guys. I made many friends with whom I was to meet up with later in various parts of the world.

There was Dicky Insall the son of a retired Senior Airforce officer, a public school character working off his national service commitment. He spoke in a well-modulated voice and smoked a Sherlock Holmes type of black carved pipe. He was great fun and was later to become a Barrister on the Midlands Circuit. Jamie Munro an ex-glider pilot, Louis (Louie) Levy who didn't smoke, drink or associate with women (as far as we could see), studied and became a fluent Malay Linguist. He was detachment commander at, I think, Jahore Baru, where his activities saw him awarded the B.E.M. He elected to end his military service in Malaya, became a Muslim and later headman of a Malay settlement. Another great friend, Ralph Thompson. A former member of the Horse Guards he regaled us with his experiences pre-war of working on a Patagonian sheep station and how they survived the bitter cold by using the bodies of dead sheep.

Then there were Sgt "Bob" Martin, John Furzer and others all with traits that made them interesting. Another mate of mine was Sgt. Derek Hopper. He also elected to take his final army discharge in Malaya. He became Security Officer on one of the largest tin mines. He later faced a murder charge but was found not guilty.

With the Emergency in full swing the Section, under HQ Malaya Command was kept busy. Civil security mobile teams went off often into the 'Ulu' (Jungle) to military units photographing, fingerprinting, and processing applicants for jobs with the forces. The Intelligence Sections in those days had very little instructions or for that matter control from HQ Malaya Command. Every now and again the FSO (Field Security Officer) would make a visit to HQ Command, and a monthly report on Military Intelligence would go to 'G' Intelligence. But few people seemed to be aware of our existence or what we did for a living. This suited us perfectly. Quite a number of incidents were taken up if thought to be interesting. We were very much a free spirit. It made for a lovely life.

At the Intelligence Centre in Maresfield they used to say there were three requirements of a Counter-Intelligence Officer. Other than training in intelligence related subjects one was required to (a) be capable of type writing a report (b) conversant with the use of a Browning automatic pistol and (c) qualified to drive a motorcycle.

I had attended, like everybody else, courses in typewriting, in pistol training and tested on a motorcycle.

So in Malaya, I typed my reports, belted on my Browning pistol, which one carried everywhere when in uniform (and often out of sight in civvies) and had a BSA 500 or another motorbike at my disposal, apart from other forms of motor transport.

One was often given a job to do and expected to be intelligent enough to carry it out without fuss.

An incident I investigated was the theft of a drug, penicillin, from the military hospital. Much prized by the local population for its use as an antidote for venereal disease it was being stolen in substantial amounts and illegally being passed to the Communist Terrorists (CTs).

One of my informants Mohd Rashid, a bit of a dodgy character, told me he thought he knew who may be involved in the theft. We needed some evidence of his suspicions so a set up was arranged whereby Rashid would invite the suspect for drinks in his house. In an adjacent room sat Dicky Insall, Dicky Moore and myself to overhear what was being said. Also with us was Chen my interpreter. Rashid had assured me the conversation would be in English but experience had indicated locals often broke into a local language especially if they became excited over a subject.

Accommodation in Malaya was designed to combat the heat. Walls were of wood with a gap at the top and bottom to allow air to circulate.

We sat at a table away from the dividing wall. Rashid had thoughtfully provided us with bottles of beer and glasses prior to the arrival of his guest.

The arrangement worked quite smoothly. Rashid brought the subject round to the penicillin drug, the conversation mostly in English. Rashid should have been an actor, he certainly earned the money given to him. It was when Rashid was escorting his guest out through the house door that a near disaster happened. Dicky I recall, making a movement of success, inadvertently knocked a beer bottle off the table. For a frozen instant all eyes followed the bottle at it headed for the floor. A hand swooped down grabbing it as it was about to land. The long fingers of Chen had saved us from mortification.

It was the start of a investigation that resulted in the arrest of hospital employees. Although no evidence of it being passed to the C.T.s was confirmed, the thefts stopped.

The Malayan climate suited me. I hated the cold all my life. I loved the hot weather. Each lunch break and most evenings we played badminton. We had the advantage of local staff who joined us and they were very good at it. Some had been semi-professionals.

Kuala Lumpur, the capital city of Malaya was a wonderful distraction. In those days, much smaller than today, its main avenue was Batu Road with brightly coloured shops and restaurants. The main meeting point for off duty 355 FSS personnel was a restaurant known as Nanto's. Owned and run by the middle aged Straits-born Chinese, Chiang Heng Fang we'd sup Mee Hoon and drink bottles of Tiger Beer.

Nanto's was also the favourite eating and drinking den of a heavily built dark skinned lady known to one and all as "Black Bess". The madam of the local street-walkers, she'd bulged like a large Buddha nightly with her brood at her favourite table, bottles of Tiger from well-wishers before her.

We became great friends. She had a boisterous sense of humour, and her knowledge of so many locals was often helpful.

Over time, often with the help of my interpreter Chen I found a useful circle of informants.

I was given the job of checking out the financial and past background of would be civilian contractors applying for military contracts. A number had worked for the Japanese during the occupation. Enquiries in 1948/49 were still ongoing into the recent past history of a number of suspected collaborators.

The Chinese triad Society also posed a problem within the ranks of the local regiments. Most criminal acts resulted from their influence.

This was my first posting to the Far East and I found Malaya a wonderful experience. Kuala Lumpur, being the capital of the country was, to me, from the colder climates, a lovely, exciting place. The population mainly of Malays, Chinese and Indians were fascinating. The rows of metal pot makers, woodworkers, paper cutters, coffin makers and so many other traders were a never ending source of interest. The noise, brightly changing colours, fragrant scents and perfume mixing with the odours of oriental cooking and spices conjured up an intoxicating land of wonder.

Entertainments were to be found also elsewhere in what I can only refer to as a colourful, noisy, bustling cross between a fairground and a circus, in which performed puppet shows, snake charmers, fire eaters, Chinese opera, dance halls, food stalls and so on in a most colourful and brightly lit noisy and fragmented world. Again, I just loved it.

Of the different populations existing side by side in this hot fascinating country I suppose my favourites were the Malays. A gentle friendly smiling race, Muslims of course. It was always a source of amusement and some embarrassment for me to eat with my Malay friends as I am left handed. For this led to continuous explanation and apologies for my actions.

Malays use their fingers to transfer food to their mouths. Their right hands are so used. Their other hand as they would explain with much amusement was to carry out more lowly tasks. Such as washing their backsides after necessary functions. I tried my best to eat with my right hand fingers but would forget and lapse into using my left hand – usually followed by a so called witty Malay friend going through the motions of washing his rear-end much to the merriment of his friends.

Another place of interest was the spacious Lake Gardens. Within it were lovely restaurants, waterfalls and beautiful birds. I remember also the Rest House, accommodations provided by the government originally for journeying government officials. Cool, spacious peaceful with an attractive dining room, they were a haven for the weary traveller.

PHOTOS: MY FAMILY

James Cambridge, my uncle, killed in action during the Dardanelles Campaign, WWI, on 24 April 1917 at the age of 27 years. He was a Sergeant in the Hampshire Regiment and is buried at the Dorian Military Cemetery in Northern Greece.

Honourable Discharge Certificate dated 10 April 1918 due to disability caused by shell shrapnel during WWI. William Hobby was my father's brother-in-law and one of my favourite uncles, a kind, and selfless man.

My father George and I.

My mother Minnie in 1943.

Barbara Dean, whom I married in 1948.

Babs and I.

My brothers and their wives at a Christmas work party. From left to right, Dennis with his wife Rose, Edna, my wife Babs, myself, my brother Eric.

Myself and Babs on our wedding day, 3 August 1948.

Outside the Registrars office following our marriage. Babs and I together with family and friends.

CHAPTER 15
355 FIELD SECURITY

During the early days of the actions with the Communist Terrorists (C.Ts) a number of quite vicious skirmishes were fought. The C.Ts were known to lay ambushes as on one particular pass on a road which led up country, shoot up the military vehicles and disappear into the jungle on both sides of the road. It provided moments of anxiety when it was necessary to travel through this pass, for many casualties both police and military and civilian were incurred until months later when the terrorists were pushed further into the jungle.

There was an occasion when I was at the railway station when I noticed a couple of soldiers talking to an Indian businessman. I noticed one of the soldiers after shaking hands with the Indian immediately put his hand in his pocket. Their actions made me suspicious. Prosperous Indian businessmen were not usually so friendly with lowly soldiers. I decided to check this a bit further. I boarded the train and persuaded the 0.C train to make me NCO 1/C train. This enabled me to travel throughout the carriages. I removed my cap badge and having located the soldiers, chatted with one of them. It turned out that they were R. Signals couriers travelling from Singapore to K.L. Making contact with my section they were interrogated by F.S and admitted using their official courier runs to smuggle raw opium for a Singapore ring. We 'turned them' and they co-operated with F.S and the police in an operation to trap the Indian but he never showed up.

A more successful matter occurred when I was

inadvertently put on the trail of a much-wanted criminal. It happened like this: in addition to using Nanto's restaurant usually with a bunch of the lads, I also, more or less as an escape from army life used another restaurant some distance away, where the food was good, had waitress service and a pleasant peaceful ambiance. It was the haunt of a number of Europeans and other ex-pats working in tin mining, rubber export and other businesses. Always in civilian clothes I gave no indication of being connected to the military. Over a period of visits I became quite friendly with one particular waitress. When things were quiet she'd sit with me and we would chat about things in general. On one occasion she mentioned her boy-friend who she said had been a 'bad boy' and had disappeared some weeks earlier. He had recently been in touch with her saying he would like to return to her and K.L. but wondered if the police were still looking for him.

This intrigued me. After a few questions I said I knew a couple of chaps in the CID, perhaps I could make some tactful enquiries to see if they had any interest in her friend. She jumped at the idea. "What's your friend's name?" I asked. Chinese names are often difficult to pronounce correctly. "Write it down, so I don't forget it." This she did and I put the note in my pocket.

Her name is long forgotten, so I will call her Lee. On the odd occasion, I had dropped Lee off at her address in the Kampong (village). These areas tend to be confusing in the dark, but taxi drivers knew their way around.

I had a chat with Capt. Masterson about the 'missing' boy-friend. He was interested. We paid a visit to the CID at police HQ in K.L. Through previous visits we were quite friendly with a number of detectives. Passing the slip of paper to them, it was obvious the name struck a chord.

It transpired the subject was something more than a "bad boy". He was wanted for blackmail, violent assault, extortion and theft and had previous convictions. The upshot was I was 'loaned' to the police to see if I could bring in the criminal.

By assuring the waitress 'Lee' the police had no interest in her boy-friend, he returned to K.L. from Penang where he had holed up.

He was now living in his girl-friend's house. It was arranged I would take Lee home from the restaurant by taxi, instruct the taxi driver to wait whilst I took her into the house and met her boy-friend, and suggest we all went out for a meal.

As back up Sgt. 'Bob' Martin was to follow me in another taxi and whilst I was in the house he was to instruct my driver to drive straight to police HQ when I returned with the girl and her boy-friend.

Things never quite go to plan.

A happy Lee and myself moved off in our taxi. Bob promptly lost us in the darkness and I didn't see him again until the operation was over.

We arrived at Lee's place in the kampong. Telling the taxi-driver to wait I accompanied Lee into the house. Sitting on her bed across the room was a squat dark coloured Chinese. There was no doubt my appearance with Lee alarmed him. Lee spoke rapidly to him in their language. He leaped to his feet at the same time grabbing a blade from a box at his feet. I pulled my Browning automatic from under my jacket and commanded him to drop the knife. He obviously knew I meant business for after hesitating he dropped it on the bed. A bewildered Lee tried to grasp what was going on "You can come with him" I said to her. "He's not going to come to any harm."

I indicated to her boy-friend to sit next to the dumb founded taxi driver with Lee sitting next to me. I instructed the driver to drive to the police HQ.

Our arrival was greeted by a smiling Captain and his

detectives. A sullen boy-friend was whisked into the cells. All the cops wanted to shake hands with me. Being a gentleman I called a taxi to take Lee home. Still bewildered, I explained her 'friend' was a lot more than a 'bad boy'. The police had also filled her in on what the thug was really like.

I gave her a hug and a kiss at the house, told her she was far better off without him, promised to see her at the restaurant and departed.

The boy-friend was sentenced to several years in prison. I was to receive $500 from the police and a commendation.

Lee didn't waste too much time getting over the boy-friend. Over a cup of tea and a few days later she confided she had a new boyfriend who was not a 'bad boy'.

It was quite amazing really, the number of jobs or enquiries we carried out which had little to do with pure security or the gathering of intelligence. One enquiry, more accurately reflecting the work we were designed to do came my way concerning an operation about to be taken against the C.Ts which was code-named "Operation Monkey".

It came to the notice of HQ Malaya Command the Communist Terrorists had somehow obtained full details of this operation. So I was sent to the Mentakab area to investigate how the classified details had been leaked.

It transpired the Commanding Officer of an Infantry Battalion was, at least, partially responsible. My report showed that in his office he had a detailed map on his office wall with full details of the operation. His office was visited by various locals at all times of the day. Unbelievably 25 civilian contractors had also been informed of details of the pending operation. Further enquiries led to two Chinese boys who were employed in the office of Kuala Lumpur Garrison Command and were working for the communists being uncovered and were imprisoned. I received a commendation for this case.

The Field Security section was allocated larger premises in KL. The new location was a beautiful house in Princes Road. It stood in its own grounds amid a large number of coconut trees. This coincided with an incident that was to put me out of action for a short while which resulted in my taking over the house as an Intelligence Centre.

It took place one lunch time. I was with the majority of the NCOs sitting in the dining room. The windows were wide and glassless. The day was hot and I was stripped to the waist. Outside in the yard which could be seen through the windows was a newly joined young National Service man who had just been instructed in the use of a motor bike. In trying to get off the bike which he had throttled down but not switched of, he overbalanced and the bike crashed to the ground and burst into flames. I, with several others leapt out of the window as someone shouted "fire". As I attempted to smother the flames our fat Chinese cook came up behind me and threw a bucket of water onto the bike. Realising what was about to happen I turned my body and face to the side. Boiling oil from the sump flew up. I felt my right arm and right side catch the oil. Running into the dining room I pulled the tablecloth off the table wrapped my arm in it and pressed it against my side. A colleague drove me to the hospital where they patched me up. It was painful…..

Returning to the unit and a most apologetic cook I took some days off and just did light duties. It was then the FSO suggested I occupy the new accommodation for the immediate future and until the move of the unit was finished. It was during my period of running the Princes

Road house I was able to make a nice little profit for the unit. One of my contacts who visited me at the house was a Chinese man who had his finger in a lot of small businesses. I suggested to him one day that perhaps he knew a chap who would be interested in purchasing the coconuts which were now ready for collection. Whether he bought them himself I don't now recall but the coconuts disappeared and I had a wad of cash in my hand which went behind the unit's bar and kept us in free drinks for quite a while.

At this time our Section Officer was a Captain "Leslie" Masterson, later to become Major. In those happy days units had their own all-rank bars. After the days work was done the so called duty NCO would be behind the bar. I recall the occasion when I was fit and well and was the duty NCO. Apart from being the barman one was the duty dogsbody. Anything that turned up, the duty NCO dealt with it.

We were having a great time in the mess. It was the weekend and the drink was flowing. That day I had been out on my new replacement bike and was still wearing DR boots. I was drinking vermouth my favourite drink at that time. How it came about I can't recall but I took on a bet which required me to drink a bottle of vermouth from one of my DR boots. All great fun until I received a phone call from a couple of our men asking for the duty NCO to come out into town and pick them up. There was nothing unusual about the request especially as they were the worse for wear from too many Saturday night drinks. So I put on my saturated boot, put drinks on the bar to keep my colleagues happy during my absence and went out to the pickup vehicle which happened to be a Dodge open backed truck.

It was necessary to drive the truck up a slope to get to the road. Of course I should never have driven but things were different in those days. In the darkness I drove the Dodge slowly forward. I had the sensation the world was slowly turning. The more I moved forward the more the world turned. I braked, opened the door and promptly fell out. Shakily I stood up. Two wheels were on the slope and two wheels off. Groggily I realised had I continued, the truck would have turned over. I wandered back into the bar. Fortunately a more sober man took the trip into town, the next day my head felt like a balloon, I decided too much vermouth wasn't good for me.

Another case that came my way concerned soldiers allegedly selling ammunition to prostitutes. Secret societies in Malay battalions were always a problem and members of clans weren't too scrupulous how they filled their pockets. The ammunition it was feared would be re-sold to C.Ts. Myself and Bob Martin were ordered to investigate.

Now our enquiries "necessitated" spending a lot of time in brothels so I talked Capt Masterson into giving me a certificate as I was a married man which stated that if I contracted VD the medical officer would be told it was caught 'In the course of duty'.

As stated earlier venereal disease was a chargeable offence with money stopped including marriage allowances. Of course I had no intention of bedding the prostitute. The document won me a few bets from unbelieving colleagues!

I was to discover many years later that all the above investigations were written about in either the Intelligence Corps magazine "the Crown and Laurel" or in other reports.

The 22 SAS were at that time situated in an isolated area not too far from Kuala Lumpur. Several SAS personnel had been involved in an incident in a local bar and Major

'Les' Masterson sent me to their unit lines to resolve the matter.

I had discussed the incident with their squadron commander and as I was about to leave, I said to the Major, "Excuse me Sir, but do you have a Lt. Woodhouse with the regiment?" the Major's eyebrows shot up. "Captain Woodhouse is unavailable," he snapped. "What would be your business with one of my officers?" "I only wished to pass on my respects," I replied. "I was with him the night he won his Military Cross." I saluted and left his tent.

Walking across the Padang, their parade ground I was hailed by a figure emerging from a tent. Capt. John Woodhouse had obviously been phoned by the major. He was pleased to see me. After a conversation concerning each other's welfare he said "Why don't you transfer to the SAS? I know your worth and would promote you to Sgt."

I politely declined his offer, saying "Thanks but as much as I know I would enjoy the move, I have now found where I want to be and I'm happy where I am."

I wasn't surprised many years later to hear he was acknowledged to be the designer of the modern and famous SAS with many operations based on the 4 man patrol unit successfully used by the 'Battle Patrol' he had commanded during the war, and to become Colonel of the SAS Regiment.

I recall an interesting but unconfirmed story of hidden treasure being discussed on one occasion in 1948 when members of 355 Field Security Section met up and had a few beers with members of 358 Section who, at that time were based further north in Malaya.

Apparently, a couple of years earlier, in 1946 a Field Security Section received information that a Japanese officer had hidden stolen treasure in the garden of his girlfriend. When Field Security Personnel investigated they found the information was correct and gold and jewellery were dug up and found to be worth millions of pounds even in those days. Then what happened to it was a bit of a mystery. Years later I was to find the story was true and had been picked up by the Straits Times and then the News of the World.

In 1946 Captain John Morton a Field Security Officer received information that Carla Wolff the Eurasian mistress of Japanese Captain Hiroshi Nakamura and who was now employed as their section clerk, had loot buried by Nakamura in her garden. Captain Morton and CSM Dawson led a raid and dug up gold, jewellery and bank notes, which in 1945, were valued at nine million pounds, concealed in petrol cans and a trunk.

Some months later Carla Wolff claimed that the personnel who had raided her house had 'misappropriated' the treasure. This led to a criminal investigation that did nothing to improve the relationship between Field Security and the Special Investigation Branch of the Military Police. CSM Dawson admitted complicity to the Special Investigation Branch. He was nearing his demobilisation date but the War Office speeded up the investigation so that CSM Dawson, Capt. Morton and another Field Security Officer Capt. Tracy could be court-martialled. The two officers were found not guilty but CSM Dawson was dishonourably discharged from the army. A SIB major was also convicted of fraudulent conversion of a currency. Captain Nakamura was later arrested by the Dutch authorities.

Quite a number of 'buried treasure' stories by senior Nazi officers were doing the rounds at the end of the war. But it was the first and only one of a Japanese Officer I ever heard of and this one turned out to be true.

CHAPTER 16
ONCE AGAIN A CIVILIAN

My time in Malaya was coming to an end. Derek Hopper had taken local discharge and had become a Security Officer at an important tin mine. I think I've mentioned elsewhere of his trial for shooting two intruders at the mine. Tried for murder he was found not guilty. I spent some pleasant days with him. I remember we found a deadly snake in his bungalow which we killed with the aid of a broom.

"Louie" Levy had also taken local leave and had settled happily in Malaya. So when I heard that a vacancy for a 'war claims Assessor and Investigator" was required by the Malayan Government I was intrigued. The pay was very good and the contract was for several years. My chances about the possibility of obtaining the position seemed very bright. I was advised I had the support of several senior officers including the Garrison Commander. Barbara, my wife, had indicated she would be happy to come out and live in Malaya.

Things were proceeding nicely when I received really bad news concerning my mother's health. She had been a diabetic for some years. As a young teenager I had often given my mother her insulin injection. Each day I'd inject into her arm or thigh with a syringe fitted with a steel needle several times thicker than they are now and nothing like as sharp. The jabs inevitably brought up a red lump around the injected spot despite how careful I was. The bad news was that they – the medical people – had discovered she had a brain tumor just before I again went overseas. Since then the tumour had grown larger and they had to operate despite her poor health. The most awful part of it was the statement made by the surgeon, that delay in operating could mean mum would become insane whilst the operation would cause complete blindness with possibly other complications.

I gave up any thought of remaining in Malaya. As soon as was possible I flew, for the first time, back to England, and having passed through the demobilisation channels I became, once again a civilian.

At that moment I believed my military service was at an end. I was wrong.

The result of my mother's operation proved to be worse than expected. She indeed lost her sight completely. What made it worse was she also lost all hearing. Fortunately although completely deaf she was able to speak and so could reply to our inquiries. After a period in hospital at Clapham South, mum was transferred to St. Benedict's hospital which was within walking distance of the family home. We were told she had not long to live, but against all odds she survived in St. Benedict's for some four years. Over time we became very adept at 'speaking' to her by writing letters in the palm of her hand, to which she was able to reply. In this way we'd converse and give her family and general news.

I had come to realise many years before that although my father was a Micawberish character and had a more optimistic outlook, my mother's view of the world was more fatalistic. By no means a pessimist she was more of a realist – and I know I take after my mother. I believe this attitude got me through the war.

To the joy of my young wife I was home! Seemingly for good. For the first few months we lived in her mother's home. On my first arrival things seemed strange. Living in her home, Babs and I were at first shy towards each other.

Understandable when you realise I'd been away for quite a while having had such a short time together. Our letters had been loving and frequent with much about how we missed each other and looked forward to the days when I would return. The shyness didn't last long. Babs had saved all the marriage allowance of the time I'd been abroad and had continued in her job. So for the first time in our young lives we had money to burn. And burn it we did! We'd never been to the West End so often before – or since. In a way we tried to make up for my absence. We were brought up short when we realised we were nearly broke. It was a salutary lesson which I have never forgotten. The savings of a couple of years evaporated in a few weeks,. I was a civilian who needed to work. And to find a place of our own.

Our first 'home' was a tiny flat in Balham. It was cold and the heating was by electric fire, maintained by putting shillings in the meter. That meter was happy. It ate shilling after shilling. We'd sit facing each other with our feet on each other's chair and a blanket over our legs. And were still cold!

I had obtained a position within the headquarters of a chain of electrical and radio outlets, starting as an accounts clerk. I was promoted to hire purchase supervisor and often attended court as the company representative in issues of substantial non-payment of money due to the company. Defendants were often represented by solicitors. By detailed study of the Hire Purchase Act I was successful in all cases.

With the help of my favourite Aunt Em I was later to buy a house. At that time I had changed jobs and to work nearer home I became an engineering inspector in a local precision engineering company with better money.

During those four years our first child Barrie was born, to the great delight of my mother. She said she had waited for a grandchild and as she cuddled this tiny baby she said she could now die happily. Indeed she passed away a few months later. Her pain, her diabetic injections and her difficulties with her disabilities were at an end, now my mother could rest in peace.

Since returning to civilian life I had tried my best to settle down. But the yearning for a more interesting life never left me. Standing, wearing the white coat of an inspector, micrometer in my hand, I'd gaze into the distance and visualised my future as a civilian. What did bug me was the awareness that having spent roughly nine years in uniform another thirteen years service would provide me with an army pension for the rest of my life.

Barbara was aware of my restlessness. We had a home and now the beginnings of a family. We were happy but she knew how I felt. We sat and discussed our future. It was agreed that I would make inquiries of the Intelligence Corps as to whether I would be able to return to the Corps. If I was accepted, I would rejoin. But I had been out of the Intelligence Corps for four years and was now over 30 years old. If unaccepted by the Intelligence Corps I would give up all thoughts of returning to military life.

I made inquiries. The reply came back. Acceptance would be subject to the results of an interview I would undergo in London. Shortly afterwards I attended an interview with an Intelligence Corps Officer. By good fortune he was an officer I had known previously. He was very friendly, had read up about me in Maresfield files and my course report of 1948. I was accepted, to be confirmed later and shook his hand.

Returning home I was happy but had some problems to resolve. Babs was excited at the idea of being an army wife at some time in the future. I put the house up for sale and sold it within a week and disposed of the contents. It had been arranged Babs and young Barrie would live with her mother until I could obtain military accommodation for us.

Returning to Maresfield and again wearing a uniform, I immediately felt at home. For a short while I was again on low privates pay. I had left as a Sergeant but I had been out too long to hold my rank. Fortunately on checking my former course report I was not required to take another, in fact for the short time I was at Maresfield I acted as an assistant instructor.

In the early months of 1955 I received my notice of services posting, unbelievable, to Singapore and Malaya!

CHAPTER 17
BACK IN UNIFORM

So for the second time and almost five years later I found myself in Singapore. I had left in 1950 with a rank of Sgt. And now I was here again in the rank of Private (Pte). This was to cause something of a problem. My posting was to the Singapore Intelligence Section and on the first evening I, with a couple of other new arrivals went to the mess to get a cold beer. Things were now different to when I was last here. The mess room was now regarded as an NCO's mess and we were told in no uncertain terms that we privates could not enter. We had to stand in the doorway until the barman condescended to bring beer over to us. We weren't too happy about this. But things were to develop.

Later, returning to the doorway for another beer, I saw the back of an officer with a glass of whisky in hand and a booming voice I recognised immediately. Maj. 'Leslie' Masterson! My old FSO. Turning, he saw me standing in the doorway. His eyebrows shot up as he recognised me. "My God! Its Cambridge!" I grinned at him. "Nice to see you again, Sir!" There was no standing on ceremony with Maj. 'Leslie'. "Come in man. Come in. Let me get you a drink." I hesitated in the doorway. There were several senior NCOs standing at the bar. Several I recognised. They didn't look best pleased. "Come in Cambridge." Leslie insisted. Actually the officer was out of order as it no longer was an all ranks mess.

Standing at the bar with a beer in my hand, I listened to Maj. Masterson talking about me to the others at the bar. Turning back to me, he said, "I can do with you back in 355 in K.L" it was then I realised he was only visiting

Singapore Section and was once again Officer Commanding the Malayan Section. I jumped at the chance of being back on my old hunting ground. "I would very much appreciate it if I could get back into Malaya," I replied. "I'll get you transferred, " Major Masterson said, sipping his whisky. "No Problem." He kept his word and a few days later I was re-posted and on my way to Kuala Lumper and meeting old acquaintances. Chen, my old interpreter was delighted to see me and in a short time I was again making contact with previous informants and old friends. Within a few days I was wearing stripes on my arm although initially they were acting ranks.

Inevitably many changes had come about since my departure in 1950. General Sir Gerald Templer had taken over as High Commissioner and Director of Operations against the Communist Terrorists (CTs) following the death of Sir Henry Gurney who was assassinated in 1951.

General Templer, who became known as "the Tiger of Malaya' (and who was to give his name to a future Intelligence Barracks at Ashford, in Kent) had successfully reduced the threat of the Communist Terrorists.

Having settled in Kuala Lumpur into the routine of Section life, my number one priority was to find accommodation for Barbara and my young son. Without confirmed and acceptable accommodation notified to the authorities the act of dispatching the family would not begin. I had the good fortune of being introduced to a long-time resident of Malaya, resident both before and after the occupation by the Japanese. Mrs. Legge was the widow of a successful and well known barrister. She had a large rambling house in beautiful gardens in which capuchin monkeys had made their home, and who provided interesting diversions to the occupants. Mrs. Legge was quite a character. Probably in her seventies she was a tough no nonsense lady who provided accommodation for junior officers awaiting military accommodations. Cpl Barry Rochford of our Intelligence Section was the person who took me along to meet Mrs. Legge. Barry, who was a bit of a 'con-man' said the way to her heart was to present her with a large bottle of gin of which she was particularly fond.

So over a few drinks the problem of my family accommodation was discussed. I discovered that the 'no-nonsense' attitude of Mrs. Legge was something of a front. She was a kind and exceedingly nice lady. She could help me out, she said, by providing accommodation of a sort. Then explained the young officers had rooms in the house but she could let me have what had been a garage at one time but had been converted in to detached living accommodation and would I like to see it. So, with a glass of gin and tonic in hand she showed me the answer to my problem.

The former garage was spacious. The front had been filled in and now had an ordinary access, and fitted with large windows. It had been subdivided into two rooms plus a bathroom, and a small kitchen. It was the answer to my problems, and in due course Barbara and son emplaned via India to Singapore and on by train to the Kuala Lumpur Rest House where we stayed for a few days before taking up residence in Mrs. Legge's accommodation.

Babs had never been abroad before and naturally found everything fascinating. Barrie was particularly taken by the capuchin monkeys, balancing on the clothes lines.

Barrie later became a favourite visitor to a restaurant in the K.L. Lake Gardens where at the age of two, in a section within the restaurant he became fascinated by a particular entertainment machine, located within an arcade of amusements. This particular activity involved him firing an electronic gun at simulated rabbits, at each successful hit a noise would sound which in turn encouraged and delighted our young son.

Visiting the shops one day in Batu Road we finished up in 'Nantos' for cold drinks. Here I found Black Bess with a beer in front of her, with her girls and introduced Barbara to her.

When we were seated I sent a bottle of Tiger over to Bess who turned and waved her thanks. Babs enquired what Bess did for a living. Her eyes widened in surprise when I told her. I suppose it is not often that a husband tells his wife an acquaintance is a madam running a team of ladies who offer their charms to one and all.

Mrs. Legge used to run a number of social events and parties to many of which we were invited. She was impatient with rank. I was careful in my decisions on which to attend. Never the less we had a number of lovely evenings when we attended occasions in which civilians from the rubber, tin mines, business men and so on were present with the District Officer and several local dignitaries.

These occasions required Barbara to appear in evening gowns and when so dressed looked quite stunning with myself in white sharkskin jacket or civilian light weight suit.

The Communist Terrorists (C.T.s) although much reduced were still active and much of our activity was occasioned by this and the security of British troops.

After some time and having reached the rank of Sergeant once again I was posted to Taiping, north of K.L. to form a detachment. With no army accommodation available this was to prove somewhat interesting on the domestic front. With a couple of junior NCOs I travelled up to survey my options.

A number of married members of the military who were serving in the area had obtained family accommodation provided by and with the local population.

But there were relatively few of these and in many cases tended to be expensive.

I struck a deal with the Chinese manager of the Hoover Hotel, whereby I was provided with a large suitable room and meals for my family at a bearable price. This enabled me to collect Barbara and young Barrie.

The Chinese manager was very friendly and went out of his way to make us happy.

The room was fitted with a large ceiling fan to combat the heat. The wooden walls between rooms had a gap of a few inches at floor level and a much larger one at the top to allow air to circulate. This led to a number of interesting incidents. The room next to ours was usually vacant as agreed with the friendly manager. But on a number of occasions it was let to short-term visitors when other rooms were occupied.

Barrie was sitting on the floor playing with his toy car when we became aware the adjacent room was occupied. Although unseen there was little doubt the male occupant had himself a female companion by the sound of a creaking bed and other indicative noises which made us stifle our giggles. It was then Barrie's wound-up car took off and before we could stop it disappeared under the wall into the next room. There was a sudden cessation of bed creaks. Suddenly the toy car reappeared. Barrie pounced on it and sensing a new game returned it from whence it came before we could stop him. We heard laughter and again the car, re-wound shot back into the room. This time I managed to grab it. A moment later a dark-skinned slim finger appeared at the bottom of the wall, making beckoning motions,. It appeared the male occupant enjoyed playing with the toy car and my son more than his other interests- at least for the moment.

Later an opportunity arose to have our own accommodation. Not exactly a 'des res' but fitting our requirements. We had had Chinese food which was pleasant to enjoy on occasions but to have it day in and day out didn't fill us with joy (Pun!)

A British NCO was about to return to the U.K. and so was vacating his civilian pad and asked if I wanted to take it on. Anything was better than that hotel room we decided and went for it.

Like most houses in the area, a wooden built house owned and lived in by a retired elderly Hindu. He had in his younger days been attached to the British Army. A number of younger relatives also occupied the house.

He was a charming old man. He was of an age which ensured he spent most of his time resting on his 'charpoy' located just inside the entrance door where he could keep tabs on the comings and goings of relatives and acquaintances.

The outgoing NCO had given me a briefing on what I would be getting for the rent I would be paying. In a nutshell the accommodation was basically the loft and was reached by a step ladder through a trap door,. For privacy and safety the trap door could be closed and locked. A window provided light.

The bungalow was situated in a large garden. Papaya and Mangosteen trees abounded. At the bottom flowed a small brook.

The furnishings in the loft were minimal but sufficient. Cooking was done on a small electric portable stove at which Barbara became quite adept. Hindu music played non-stop from a radio on the floor below. We got quite used to it and became familiar with many of the tunes.

The Hindu family were very friendly and Barrie became a great favourite often spending time in the safe company of 'Kichi' a young son of the family.

I remember looking for my young son one meal time. He was not to be found in the garden. Walking to the end of the garden I saw him with Kichi squatting on the bank of the small stream, Barrie was crouching in the few inches of water endeavouring to catch tiny fish with a condensed milk tin. Clad only in shorts he was completely engrossed in his fishing.

We lived there for several months. Life was pleasant, and the work was not too arduous. An incident of little importance I did have to deal with and I reported on in my monthly report to Section HQ I've entered here:

Ghost Hunter – A report came in that the locally employed staff at a senior officer's residence were reluctant to work in the building because it had become haunted. They believe it had a ghost. Slow footsteps and mysterious tappings above their heads was frightening them out of their wits and they wanted to bring in a medicine man (bomo) to remove the ghost. Aide de Camp contacted us. Judicious enquiries and friendly approaches by a tactful FSS NCO resulted in the following.

A British army soldier whose duties were either batman or driver or both – I can't recall- idled away the more boring periods of his day by taking advantage of a double staircase to the first floor. He would slip into the house, up the stairs, don a pair of ammo boots, slowly and heavily move across the floor making appropriate noises, hide the boots and disappear out of the house using the other staircase

A warning of a dire future resulting in the extraction of a promise from the grinning soldier to henceforth desist from scaring the living daylights out of the locals ensured the visit and incantations of the 'Bomo' when he entered the residence were completely successful and the 'bantu' (ghost) was banished forever.

Finally the day came with the good news we had been allocated military accommodation. The entire Hindu family came out to wish us farewell and presented Barbara with a beautiful bunch of flowers. With Barrie waving vigorously we moved off to our new and final accommodation in Taiping.

It was whilst living here my second child made his appearance. Driving to the military hospital on hearing my second son was born, I found a happy but tired Barbara. Following the usual congratulations and embraces I looked for the baby to be told he had been returned to another room for a while to give mother a break. A nurse took me to see my new son. I peered in the cot at the tiny figure, red of face and sleeping peacefully. I looked around, at a number of other cots. I looked again at my sleeping child. "He's got hair on his chin", I said. The nurse smiled and said "That's only fluff. It will be gone in a couple of days". As we moved away I glanced into the other cots, in each was a sleeping child. All had dark skin, all were Gurkha children. Mark, as my son was to be named, was the only child of British parents to be born that day at that military hospital in Kamunting, Taiping, Malaya. It was Christmas Eve. Four hours later and he would have been a Christmas day child. For his parents he was a wonderful, joyful, gift!

Here the section carried out its duties of military installation checks and other duties. Again we made life pleasant for ourselves. We would have the occasional visit by the Field Security Officer (FSO), but other than preparing the monthly intelligence report we were able to plan activities to suit ourselves.

Later I was to take over the Penang Detachment. Of all the various detachments this was acknowledged as being the best. Located the furthest north, it was a most beautiful holiday resort, a one man detachment at the time which required me to do my own legwork. This suited me fine. Much of my work was to liaise with the various service units in the north of the country. This was to be a great help when a spot of bother needed to be dealt with later.

On a previous tour I had spent a restful break with my colleague Derek Hopper on Penang Island. It was just after he had been acquitted on a murder charge whilst carrying out his duties on a civilian tin mine.

Lying on sun beds, served with John Collins and watching the steamers moving through the warm sea, we had reflected life couldn't get much better.

On this present posting life was again enjoyable. Then the phone rang. Major 'Les' Masterson, my FSO. "Ah Cambridge. Have a little job for you. An Australian soldier has lost his FN rifle overboard whilst travelling back to his regiment from Penang on the ferry. Look into it. Loss of rifle is a court-martial offence."

I put the phone down. What did he mean 'Look into it'. Did he just want a report, or what? First requirement was to get the facts. Visiting the Australian infantry battalion I interviewed the worried soldier and others who had been present when the rifle disappeared overboard. Seemed the soldier had rather stupidly leaned his weapon against a stanchion on the side of the ferry as he lit up a cigarette whilst talking to his companions. The boat had 'jarred' as a wave hit it, dislodging the weapon which slipped through an aperture into the sea.

It transpired the weapon was undergoing trials before becoming the replacement weapon for the infantry which indicated the soldier should have taken even more care of it than usual.

The incident had taken place on a Sunday and I was dealing with the matter the following day. I obtained the approximate time the soldier had been travelling, when the rifle went overboard, and other details.

Back on Penang Island I collected other information from the ferry authorities, time of tides, indication of line of travel and so on. The ferry was making the crossing from Penang to Butterworth, a distance of eight or nine miles.

I considered the possibility of recovering the weapon. To do so I would need divers, although the possibility of recovery seemed remote. Then I had a spot of luck, asking around my contacts, I was to hear that a group of RAF men were believed to do a bit of amateur diving.

The RAF were stationed on the mainland. Travelling over to Butterworth I made contact with an air force liaison officer who made it possible to speak to a more senior officer.

Thanking him for seeing me, I explained the situation, and then brought up the subject of the airmen who did diving as a hobby. The officer indicated he didn't think much of any recovery chances but went on to say, "Yes, I'm aware a number of my men have formed a group who dive for their own pleasure. If they wished to do so in this instance it would be entirely their own choice and would be in their own time." He then gave me names and rank of several airmen and how to make contact.

To be frank there isn't a lot that airman and 'brown jobs' i.e. army personnel have in common, but on introducing myself and explaining what I was about they became intrigued with the idea. Several said they were up for it and it was agreed the action would take place the coming Sunday.

The group would travel over to Penang at a specific time when I would meet them. I would arrange boats and would take care of any expenses they may incur.

During the week I arranged to rent two boats with their Malay skippers and decided on where the rifle was likely to be and took sightings on which to line the boats. Sometimes I thought the matter seemed to verge on the ridiculous with the chances of recovery absent. But I thought I'd give it my best shot anyway.

Come the Sunday, everything came together nicely. The airmen came on time with their bits and pieces, the boatmen were standing by and at the appropriate time we moved into the Strait of Malacca.

We hovered in the area I had judged the rifle had entered the sea. The sun shone, the sea was calm and I watched as the divers, two at a time splashed into the sea and at times changed places with each other. Then, unbelievably it happened. On his third dive an airman came to the surface. As he broke through the water surface he was holding aloft a long object. It was the rifle! Moments later it was with me in the second boat. It had been on the bottom of the sea for seven days yet barnacles were already forming on the metal. But it had been recovered. Unbelievable!

The following day I returned it to the Australians much to their surprise and delight. It had saved one of their kind from a court-martial.

When I reported back to Major Masterson on the successful recovery, he said "Good-oh, the Aussies now owe me a bottle of whisky."

When I entered my monthly report I included a detailed breakdown of expenses incurred. A slight inflation ensured that if Major 'Leslie' was getting a bottle of whisky then I at least deserved a beer or two!

In 1955 Major Masterson FSO was visiting Singapore Field Security Section. At some time in his varied past he had killed a crocodile. Trouble was he never stopped talking about it. Whenever he was at a Mess Bar and had a whisky or two the audience would once again hear of this astounding incident of how he had killed this denizen of the deep. Whether the length of the monster increased with the telling of the tale, we were never to know for he was silenced once and for all after he had again recounted how he had slain the crocodile. Picking up his glass of whisky he said "45 feet long, it was". At this moment Ron Rae, who was acting barman, came from behind the bar, tugging a piece of string. Out came a tatty stuffed 15 foot long crocodile. Innocently he asked "Was this the one, Sir?"

PHOTOS: MY FIRST TWO MALAYAN POSTINGS

Frank Furzer of 355 Field Security Section, someone with too much free time on their hands!

Eddie 'Bob' Martin, 'On Parade'.

Derek Hopper and friends. 1950, Malaya.

Frank Furzer, Eddie 'Bob' Martin, Louis Levy, Dickie Sweetman. May 1949, Malaya.

Derek Hopper. Malaya, 1949.

Members of 355 Field Security Section. Port Dickson, Malaya.

H.Q. 355 Field Security Section. Kuala Lumpur, Malaya.

Lake Gardens. Kuala Lumpur, Malaya.

Kuala Lumpur Rail Station.

Sampans in Malacca Harbour.

The day following the motorcyde incident. Having a few beers to keep my strength up.

Reg on the beach in Malacca, December 1949.

Following medical advice not to work too hard. June 1949, Kuala Lumpur, Malaya.

Enjoying some of the many social occasions hosted by Mrs Legge.

The Cambridge family: Reg, Babs, Barrie and Mark. 1957, Taiping, Malaya.

Sergeant Reginald Cambridge at 355 Field Security Section. 1948, Kuala Lumpur, Malaya.

Lt. Colonel John Woodhouse as Commanding Officer of 22nd Special Air Service Regiment.

CHAPTER 18
HOLLAND & GERMANY POSTINGS

When my Malayan posting ended and returned to U.K. I was placed on the staff of HQ at Maresfield for a few months. Before taking over the detachment at the Hook of Holland. It was another out of the way job. Although spoken of as a 'Detachment' it was the only Dutch posting at the time for the Intelligence Corps, with myself as Detachment Commander the only other member a Corporal.

A detachment also existed in Antwerp, Belgium which was 'a one man band' liaison outfit held by a colleague Gus Ford. Maintaining contact with the port officials, meeting the odd VIP on his way to the armed forces in Germany and liaising with the few British units located nearby didn't stretch me. On occasions I drove to Antwerp and met up with Gus which went down on my monthly report as a 'liaison' visit.

We, that is Barbara, Barrie, Mark and myself had accommodation in a very nice house with pleasant Dutch neighbours and had the services of a cleaner who became a friend of the family. Two members of the Dutch Security Forces became great friends, often visiting our home for a game of chess. Very Pleasant.

A dreadful incident which occurred on the nearby beach remains in my mind. It is to be remembered the war had been over for some twelve years. I recall I was parking the unit Volkswagen at the office when a massive explosion hit my eardrums. A column of black smoke showed the location to be at the beach.

Scrambling back into the car I was quickly at the beach to find a large hole in the sand. Parts of a human body were scattered across the area. Later other body parts were to be removed from the roof of a nearby building.

The cause of the explosion was established. A land mine, unearthed in the sand by the action of the tide, had been stumbled across by a group of young Dutch men. None of them were aware of what it could be. Looking at it and discussing possibilities one of the four produced a screwdriver or some other tool. His three companions became alarmed and when the young man declared it could be worth money as scrap metal they warned the youth of possible danger and put distance between the metal object and themselves. This action saved their lives. It seems the young man touched or inserted the tool at which action the mine exploded, the man taking the full force of the detonation.

At his funeral it was rumoured sand bags were put in his coffin to make up for the weight of missing body parts.

Gus Ford phoned me. "Hi Reg. I've got just the car for you and at a good price." He knew I was driving around in the unit's Volkswagen and hadn't bothered to obtain a car of my own. "What are you on about" I replied. "Well, you know I've got this lovely Ford Vedette and I'm offering it to you at a special low price."

"Not interested," I said. "It's too big for me and anyway I'm not wanting a car at this time." I sensed his voice had an anxious note in it. The penny dropped. "Are you being posted?" I asked, with a grin. "Well, yes." He admitted. "They've cut this posting short and I think I may be off to the Far East."

"Sorry, Gus can't help you. What do I want with a bloody big car with a V8 engine, it will cost a fortune to run."

I knew the car. Large, black, reminiscent of cars favoured by American gangsters in films. The next day

Gus was back on the phone. He was now pleading with me. I knew he was in something of a cleft stick for I knew if he had bought the car under rules favouring the British occupying powers in Europe he could only pass it to another Brit if he had not had it for a specific period of ownership.

"Reg, come on. Help me out, I've got to unload the car within a week or I shall be in real trouble." He pleaded.

"Sorry, Gus. I'm not fond of big cars or their maintenance costs." I said.

The next day Gus was again on the phone. "I'm reducing the price specially for you," he stated. I interrupted him. "Look, I know you are in a bind so I'll make you a special offer, I've always liked the radio in your car. I'll offer you fifty quid for the radio, providing you throw the car in!"

H was annoyed "Not likely!" he bellowed down the wire and slammed the phone down.

I grinned to myself. I was enjoying this. I felt in a funny way I was getting my own back for the incident when I was put in my place at the Sgt's Mess in Singapore a couple of years earlier when I had to stand in the door way and ask the barman for a beer. Gus Ford had been one of the senior NCO's who had looked down on the new arrivals which had included me.

Time was running out for Gus and I awaited another phone call. It came. "Ah, Reg" his voice admitted defeat. "OK, you can have it for 50 quid. I haven't much choice, have I?" I silently gave a thumbs up. But I wasn't quite finished.

"We have a little problem here, Gus" I said. "You are in Belgium and I'm here in Holland. I've a few jobs on at the moment and can't get down to your end. Now you know I'm a generous guy, you drive the Ford up here to the Hook and I'll give you lunch and drive you to the rail station where you can catch a train back."

The following day I waved him goodbye. I wasn't to meet up with Gus for quite a while but when we did I found he hadn't forgotten.

The car was a joy to drive. I drove the family to many interesting places in Holland. Later, when posted back to the Intelligence Centre at Maresfield it paid its way despite its petrol thirst. Visits to relatives were a delight and all were impressed with the car. Later, when I was due to be posted I flogged it to a couple of young soldiers who practised their driver training by driving it around the roads of the camp, until one whacked it into a tree. What they did with it I never did find out. By then I was overseas again.

It was whilst stationed in Holland our third and last child was born. The British forces had an arrangement with the Dutch authorities whereby the occasional birth of a British subject was taken care of in the Hague at a Medical Centre named the 'Emma Klinik'.

The birth was interesting in that the local driver of the ambulance taking a heavily pregnant wife and myself became lost in the outskirts of 'Den Hague'. With time passing and the birth becoming more likely by the minute a frantic driver asked a series of passers-by who shook their heads on being asked the location of the 'Klinik'. Finally somebody gave him directions but he again became lost in a busier section of the city and Barbara agonisingly hanging on warned me the birth was becoming imminent.

Finally the perspiring driver found the right location and I immediately raced into the clinic saw a nurse and blurted out the situation. The nurse smiled and calmly said she would deal with the pregnant lady and collecting Barbara from the ambulance conducted her up a flight of stairs.

It seemed it was only seconds later when the nurse raced to the staircase calling me to come quickly. It was the first and only time I actually attended the birth of any of our children. The doctor and nurses were first class, joking amongst themselves, all in English. With the success of Barbara's exhausting effort and the doctor cradling a British girl, who we were to name Wendy, a nurse remarked I looked exhausted, sat me down and brought me a glass of beer.

A proud mother, holding our baby claimed she needed it more than I did!

The day came with my last posting to Europe, initially taken on strength at HQ, Rheindahlen, I was pleased to be posted to 14 Detachment at Dortmund, only to find my detachment commander none other than Gus Ford from whom I had purchased that Ford Vedette when in Holland.

He hadn't forgotten either. Meeting up with him on my arrival I could see he was mentally rubbing his hands at the prospect of getting even for my holding him 'over a barrel' on my purchase of his car. "Ah, Reg! Good to see you again," he grinned as we shook hands.

For the next few weeks I caught every boring job he could find to put my way. Every security survey, particularly night checks – every required visit to HQ- every immediate report required to be prepared, all came my way. Finally, during a conversation whilst waiting for the arrival of our German Special Branch contacts I brought up the subject of all the extra work he had been loading on me. "Fair do's" I said. "I reckon all this work you've been piling on me should make up for the car incident. After all I lost money on it when I had to sell it." I said. He grinned "I've been thinking about that. I tell you what; I've had an idea in my head for a while. If you

are willing to come in on it with me, we will call it quits."
He then went on to say he had been thinking of setting up a club to enable us to fire hand held arms. Dortmund Pistol Club. He already had a name for it. "Help me set it up," he said. I knew Gus was a keen pistol shot. He'd visited various outlets purchasing under-arm holsters and other artefacts connected with hand guns. I was interested. Although not as fanatical as Gus on the subject of handguns, being a good shot with pistol, revolver and for that matter, rifle I was quite taken with the idea. I agreed to go into it with him and with the help of our local police friends we obtained the use of a gallery. With the Dortmund Pistol Club formed we invited members of the local CID, Special Branch and several members of other organisations to become members and arranged special monthly meetings. This turned out to be a very good way of establishing friendships and whereas in the past we had had a good relationship with local organisations in a number of cases this turned into personal friendships.

On one occasion Gus and I were invited to join K-14, a department of Special Branch, on their annual "Mystery Tour". Each year a small committee was formed who decided how their annual police day was to be spent. Until the day, activities were kept under wraps.

On this occasion Gus and I joined our friends at the modern police HQ. I always remember the lifts. They were without open and closing doors, moved slowly up and down sufficiently to allow access and departure. Two lifts, one moving continuously up and the other continuously down. Quite smart.

A bar had been set up and as we arrived a schnapps glass was pressed into our hands. The glass was carried throughout the day and at the command of 'Schnapps!' which was frequent, one had to stand to attention with the glass held forward to be filled. The committee man with the bottle was soon filled with his own offering and staggered throughout the day in a happy cloud of merriment, whilst each of the two Englishmen tried to avoid catching his eye.

The mystery tour we discovered was a day trip along the River Rhine. Food and drink was continuously available, the weather was fine and the schnapps ensured everybody was in an enjoyable mood. The evening was spent in a Kebel Bowling Club. This was also a monthly meeting place of the German Special Branch. Gus and myself were made honorary members. The club took place in the cellar of a 'bierstube'. At one end stood nine wooden pins, to which you rolled a wooden ball along the lines of 10-pin bowling. Scores were counted and losers paid in beer. At the other end a large table with probably twenty or so chairs dominated the room. Here the Kebel Meister announced birthdays of those present, and pronounced on other subjects relevant to the existence of the club. Each birthday or other announcement was met with loud table hand thumping by his audience and with much imbibing from steins of beer. I must say our friends had a propensity to sink large quantities of the foaming ale, causing a few problems for their English guests. Gus, I found could get tipsy on a couple of drinks and quite rightly tried to avoid it as much as possible. But at these bowling evenings it was difficult to avoid. Gus would switch steins with mine which made my problems worse. On these evenings I would prepare myself by drinking milk to coat my stomach. We also arranged for a unit driver to stand by to drive us to our respective homes.

Discussing the day later, Gus and I considered we had an obligation to repay our friends in one way or another. Our Detachment of some half a dozen military personnel occupied the wing of a former German barracks. It was decided our response would be in the form of a cocktail party. We arranged a four piece group to provide back ground music. Several of the junior ranks offered to wait upon our guests. In the large room we moved in appropriate furnishings. Supplies of food stuff and drink was in abundance. Making up some strong cocktails I recall dipping the rims of glasses in refined sugar which became rather popular.

In those post-war days it appeared to us our German friends enjoyed much of their leisure in the company of colleagues. This of course is understood. But we gained the impression that having the company of their wives on such occasions appeared to be rare.

When we printed the invitation cards we made them out to 'Herr and Frau'. At that time the only married couples of the detachment were the two senior NCOs, Gus and myself. We decided not to have the wives along. We could pay more attention to working the room.

The cocktail party was a success. In fact it was a roaring success going on long into the evening. Naturally we paid much attention to the wives. Initially slightly apprehensive, this quickly disappeared after sampling our 'highly recommended' cocktails. Cigarettes were available on side tables and I was intentionally available to offer a light from my cigarette lighter to the delighted ladies. I was hence forth referred to as 'Herr Feurman'. We were to hear from our German colleagues how they all enjoyed the party, particularly their woman folk.

The political atmosphere had made changes in many of our intelligence activities. For this was in the long period referred to as the 'Cold War'.

One of our duties involved line crossers from East Germany. Each case was interrogated to define whether one was an escapee from the East or had crossed with an ulterior motive.

A task I also carried out was the physical inspection of nuclear war heads poised ready for action toward the east.

For this I was provided with a special security vetting clearance of a particular code name. The inspections were carried out by a team made up of representatives from Intelligence units from USA, Germany, Canada and Britain.

The Cold War ensured we had a busy but interesting life.

CHAPTER 19
MALAYA, HONG KONG & END OF SERVICE

With my wife and three children we departed the U.K. en-route for Singapore, and my favourite location – Malaya. During the last few years changes had come to this part of the world. The political scene had changed. 'Merdeka' – Freedom had at last been obtained. Malay's now controlled their own destiny.

Married family quarters were not immediately available and we were accommodated temporarily in the Seremban Rest House. I've mentioned Rest Houses before, beautiful and spacious they were quite comfortable. Here we met up with another couple awaiting family accommodation. Brian a Warrant Officer in one of the logistical units had recently married Lee. They became close friends. (Today they live in France and we are still in contact with each other.)

By good fortune we became neighbours when we were allocated attractive bungalows within the Seremban Military Base. Whilst the men were carrying out their respective military duties, the wives could often be seen reclining on cushioned bamboo chairs and shaded from the sun on the bungalow verandahs. The children became great favourites with Lee. Mark was a particular favourite despite firing his rubber tipped arrows at the ladies.

The Communist Terrorists (C.T.s) had to all intents been defeated, and no longer threatened the inhabitants. Things were also changing in the use of formations of our units. The old 355 Field Security Section had gone and in its place was the Counter Intelligence Platoon Malaya. But organisations were in a state of flux and it wasn't long before – without any change that I could see – I was part of an Intelligence company, Seremban Section. A number of Malay Intelligence Corps, recently set up were attached to us.

The Malays were very pleasant although they did have the unexpected habit of holding one's hand when going into town together... our activities were now confined to the British units stationed around. There is no denying life was very pleasant. I purchased the former District Officer's car – a large Fiat 2000cc – when he returned to the U.K. the family enjoyed trips to Port Dickson and other holiday resorts. They also became excellent swimmers thanks to instructions from an army physical training instructor. A large pool and a NAAFI store was available to British personnel.

Half way through my Malayan tour I suddenly received notice of posting to Hong Kong. I was to discover an old friend of mine RSM Harry Dunn had been taken seriously ill and was being returned to the U.K. I suppose I was the nearest Warrant Officer to Hong Kong and so I was required to take over as Company Sgt Major of the Intelligence and Security Section, Hong Kong, at short notice.

We packed and moved to Singapore where we embarked on a Hercules aircraft. I recall we had twelve suitcases. Also on the plane were a number of Gurkha soldiers who quite willingly assisted the family.

The interior of the aircraft which usually moved bulk stores was pretty basic. Moving around heavy netting we settled into netting seats. The children were quite excited by all the activity. The plane zoomed into the air and headed for Hong Kong airport which in those days was Kai-Tak. It was known as a tricky airport at which to land. Planes had to fly over mountains and the part of Hong

Kong known as Kowloon to be faced with a steep descent over high-rise blocks of accommodation. The landing strip was facing out to sea and surrounded by water. Later, we were to see a plane land badly and shoot off the landing strip into the sea. A ship was always on hand for such an emergency. I believe one elderly lady was the only fatality dying from a heart attack.

We found we had been allocated a flat recently vacated by a married NCO. It is standard practice in the Armed Services for army quarters to be inspected on march out for cleanliness. This one hadn't. It was a private flat rented by the Armed Services and had fallen through the net regarding inspection. Barbara exhausted by the children and the journey collapsed on the bed in tears. At first I thought the flat was untidy then as I checked the rooms I found it much worse and when I discovered decomposing fish heads behind the cooker and the interior of the fridge dirty I blew my top. I found out who was the NCO responsible for the inspection, wheeled him into the flat and said I was about to make a written complaint to the authorities. The shaken NCO said he would locate the previous occupant and make him bring the place up to an acceptable standard. Meanwhile I put the family in a nearby hotel. The angry Quarter Master Sgt brought in the NCO and wife much to their chagrin and the flat was thoroughly cleaned. Later, after I had accepted the flat in its new condition we had the good fortune of being offered accommodation in a far better location and on the seventh floor of a block of flats with a wide verandah at Kowloon Tsai, overlooking the bay and the airport. Sitting on the verandah one could see every rivet on the underbody of the planes as they descended barely missing the roof of the flats levelling out sharply just before reaching the landing strip. It was mesmerising as it seemed unlikely the pilot would make it. It was on this verandah I saw the aircraft bounce into the sea resulting in the death of the old lady. (later the Chinese built a 'State of the Art' airport at Chek Lap Kok and as far as I know Kai-Tak became redundant.)

Hong Kong is known as 'the Pearl of the Orient' a fascinating place, controlled in those days as a British outpost with the Island capital of Victoria. A number of specialist Intelligence Corps personnel, such as Photographic Interpreters (P.I.) were stationed on the Island which was connected to the mainland by a Ferry Service. The main body of the Intelligence Group were on the mainland in barracks at Kowloon. Towards the border with China proper the area was known as the New Territories. Here observation posts kept an eye on the Chinese troops who of course were doing the same with us!

Our duties allowed for plenty of time off, walking the narrow lanes and watching the Chinese industrially at work was quite fascinating. Guitar and violin makers were my special fascination. The intense absorption and speed of their hands was unbelievable. To the rear of our block of flats were steep hills, one known as Bun Rock. It rose steeply with a narrow path along its spine. The children would race up and down this path despite instruction to slow down. I had never been afraid of heights but I've since come to the conclusion the exploits of Mark and Wendy whooping and dancing along this climbing narrow track, making my heart come into my mouth and a strong risk of a heart attack is the cause of dislike of heights in my old age!

So time passed pleasantly and seemingly far too quickly. With time running out we visited the NAAFI and the town to purchase last minute gifts for those at home. Passing a stand of golf clubs in the NAAFI and thinking it would be a nice idea to take up the game sometime in the future but knowing nothing about the clubs I took the advice of a salesman and purchased a set.

Sometime later back in England I took a few lessons only to find that I had purchased a set of "blades" it was explained to me these clubs are far better in the hands of well experienced golfers and were not for the high handicapper! They stayed hidden in the cupboard until I decided to take up golf and joined a club at the age of seventy eight disposing of those and purchasing more user friendly clubs! I'm still a high handicapper!

When my current overseas tour was up I found I had been allocated married quarters in Howe Barracks, Canterbury, Kent. Whilst I had been abroad the Intelligence Corps Headquarters had moved from Maresfield, Sussex to Ashford in Kent.

Harry Dunn and his family were in quarters nearby. He had cancer and I was advised his life expectancy was limited. I was requested to provide all assistance to Harry and his family which I was of course pleased to do. Although his wife, who was German was aware of the severity of his condition, I'm not so certain Harry had been told. I'd sit with him and he would seem unaware of his true situation. He would talk about his future and what his ambitions were. Harry was a great chap. I'd known him most of the time I had been in the Corps and his situation was keenly felt. I was given plenty of time off what with disembarkation leave and so on. Technically I was put in charge of the Rapid Response Group. Its duties were in its nomenclature, ready to go anywhere at short notice.

Harry succumbed to his illness rather suddenly. He was given a military funeral and buried at Highgate Cemetery, made famous by Karl Marx being buried there. I was one of the coffin bearers. A house was found for the family and for many years I kept in touch.

During this time I had myself been feeling unwell. In

fact I had been feeling pretty rough for quite some time. The medical officer thought I may be anaemic and I began a series of interviews at several hospitals. Finally I was diagnosed with having 'Tropical Sprue' a celiac type of condition, and was hospitalised at Milbank Military Hospital, where I was told I had probably had the condition for over two years, since Malaya. I had been losing weight. It had taken some time to confirm the condition and a medical board downgraded me. Although technically I could have soldiered on for another five years, I had come to the conclusion my time in the service was coming to a close. My children were now in their teens or approaching it.

I chauffeured Barrie my eldest son to Ashford Grammar School when I was available and it was when trying to find a country route from Canterbury to avoid the main route to Ashford I was to discover a country property which was to become our home for many years to come.

My service had not quite finished though. During 1970/71 the threat of the activities of the IRA in Northern Ireland were very real. I was instructed to take a team and carry out a series of assessments of certain vulnerable points (V.P.) and write up detailed reports. I recall locations included Harland and Wolf, certain gas and oil refineries and other installations. We were given six weeks to get the job done.

The team did a great job. At each location I would present the draft survey to the management for opinion and accuracy. It was pleasing to hear the assessments. I recall the General Manager of a particular refinery on reading our survey report and conclusions remarking he had college graduates on three year training programmes who knew less about the installation than we had obtained in a matter of weeks!

Back at HQ Intelligence Corps, I had applied to leave the services. The whole business of discovering I had Tropical Sprue to the final medical board had taken some four months.

The day came when I finally became a civilian for the third and last time. Some thirty years had passed since I had asked that recruiting officer for my first ever 48 hour pass. I had spent most of the war years and much of peacetime in khaki. The authorities had, over the years graded my conduct from 'good' to 'very good' and now, finally 'exemplary'!

One cannot forget their past. Now, having reached a respectable age being aware of friends and comrades passing on, I appreciate fate has been kind to me and I am a fortunate man. I remember them with sadness, but great affection and am honoured to have known them.

PHOTOS: HONG KONG POSTING

'Bun Rock' with the hills of 'Lion Rock' behind. The view from the rear balcony walkway of our apartment at Kowloon Tsai.

'Stonecutters Island'. Used by families of British Forces as a place for fun, activities and relaxation. A small Island a short boat-ride from Hong Kong.

The New Territories. Where Hong Kong's border with China existed before the Territories lease with the UK expired.

A Junk heading towards Kowloon Bay.

Nathan Road, Kowloon. A busy, exciting, colourful retail centre in Downtown Kowloon.

A regular image of aircraft preparing to land at Kai-Tak airport, flying close to high-rise commercial and residential buildings in Kowloon during the 60's before its closure.

PHOTOS: THE CHILDREN

Barrie, Mark and Wendy at home in Dortmund, West Germany. 1964.

Mark, Wendy and Barrie in Scotland. August, 2012.

Mark and Wendy ready to fish at Port Dickson, Malaya, with Babs beside them.

Mark and Wendy going to the pool in Seremban Barracks, Malaya. 1966.

Barrie, Wendy and Mark on the beach.

PHOTOS: REUNITED AFTER 60 YEARS

Reg and Dennis Scaife in Dorset, having reunited after 60 years.

Babs, Reg and Dennis Scaife swapping stories and relaxing in Buckinghamshire.

Dennis Scaife at home in Adelaide, Australia.

Dennis and Reg. Old pals happy together.

Dennis Scaife visiting his old Commanding Officer, John 'Charlie' Woodhouse from 60 years ago, at a nursing home in Dorchester, UK.

John Woodhouse with grandchildren, Alex and Lucy.

ACKNOWLEDGEMENTS

My thanks are due to Petrina, daughter-in-law for her time and effort in deciphering my badly written hand writing and transforming it into understandable prose. Also for her interest and persuasion in coaxing me to continue writing when I flagged.

For the support and advice provided by Mark my son over many months I record my appreciation and many thanks.

Sincere thank you also to my grandson Stephen for his technical assistance in arranging the design and publication of this book.

My thanks are also due to Michael Woodhouse for the use of Copyright, photographs of his father Lt. Col John (Jock) Woodhouse and to Debbie and her family for the use of photos of her father, Dennis Scaife.

The Imperial War Museum and the Surrey Infantry Museum who kindly permitted use of copyright material, as did The War Graves Photographic Project (TWGPP).

APPENDIX I
REST IN PEACE

This book is inspired and dedicated to the memory of three individuals whom I was grateful to have known and be considered as their friend and fellow Battle Patrol colleague; John 'Charlie' Woodhouse, Dennis Scaife and Eric Monsey.

Although now passed on, you all forever live in my thoughts.

APPENDIX II
DENNIS LIONEL SCAIFE

When I rejoined the Army in 1947/48, I lost contact with Dennis (Lou) Scaife. Over the years I often wondered how he was making out. Then nearly 60 years later whilst living in Buckinghamshire I received a letter from 'Friend Finders' a search organisation, stating a Debbie Scaife was searching for a war-time friend of her father. The only information she could provide was his name, Reg Cambridge, who had married a girl named Babsie. It seems I was one of a handful with that name.

Making contact with the agency I subsequently spoke to a delighted Dennis who said his daughter had spent ages online and other channels trying to find me.

He went on to say he, with his wife Iris emigrated to Australia a few years after the war ended, had seven children and now in his retirement would be delighted to come over to the U.K. to meet up with his old buddy.

Many emails, phone calls and letters followed and a delighted Debbie said she was over the moon having located her dad's old pal. She said her mom had passed away three years earlier leaving a heart broken, depressed Dennis and making contact with me had re-vitalised him.

Several weeks later whilst sitting reading a book, the doorbell rang. Babs came back into the room and announced I had a visitor. I looked up to see the lanky, grinning form of my old friend. I recognised him immediately. "Lou!" I exclaimed. "Lou's long gone, its Dennis now" I was told.

It was hard to believe so many years had passed, it was though we hadn't been apart and he was still the cheerful, ever smiling corny joke teller.

He had booked into nearby accommodation which I insisted he cancel and stay with us and apart from a week he spent with his brother still living in the U.K, we were inseparable.

We drove down to Dorset and made a number of visits to Castle View Nursing Home where our old Battle Patrol Commander (Lt. Col. John Woodhouse MBE MC, Ret.) was a resident. In his later years he suffered from Parkinson's disease and curvature of the spine. He had remained in the army after the war and led an exciting and sometimes a 'cloak and dagger' life in the SAS and the War Office and we had met several times during peace time service.

Our former O.C.'s comment on our first meeting was "How is it whenever I see you, you are always together?" Despite the passing years and subsequent varied lives, the Battle Patrol days were well remembered. 'Charlie' Woodhouse and Dennis swapped stories of their times as POWs and we heard interesting incidents of life in the SAS.

The following year Dennis again came over to the U.K. and spent an extended holiday with us and again we went off to Dorchester and the local area and made further visits to John Woodhouse who we discovered was something of a practical joker hiding the trolley of a confused tea lady.

It seemed ironic that having met up after all those years apart it was to be short lived, for after returning home to Adelaide Dennis was found to have cancer and in 2006 my old pal passed away.

His daughter Debbie, tells me he is buried next to his beloved wife Iris, and on the headstone over his grave is inscribed 'Dennis The Menace'.

APPENDIX III
LT. COL. JOHN WOODHOUSE MBE MC

Lt. Col. John Woodhouse joined the 1st Battalion the East Surry Regiment during the Tunisian Campaign in February 1943. In the subsequent Italian Campaign Lt. John Woodhouse commanded the Battalion Battle Patrol which at full strength numbered sixteen.

Many sorties were carried out on and behind German lines often for periods of several days resulting in the award of the Military Cross to 'Charlie' Woodhouse as he was known to his men.

During 1947-49 he studied Russian at Cambridge and was an Interpreter with the Control Commission in Germany. In 1958 he transferred to the Parachute Regiment and in 1962 he was chosen to command 22 SAS Regiment.

Colonel David Stirling founder of the SAS acknowledged John Woodhouse as a co-founder of the modern SAS, who he stated had restored it to its original philosophy with his grasp of how men should be selected, trained and directed for Special Forces, drawing on his experience with the Battle Patrol revolutionised the SAS and helped overcome Communist Terrorists in Malaya and confrontation with Indonesia. David Stirling and John Woodhouse subsequently provided advice and guidance on training of their Special Forces to the U.S. Military.

Upon retirement he joined the family brewery of Hall and Woodhouse in Dorset where he took the small loss making Sunparlour Soft Drinks Company into profit with the introduction of 'Panda Pops' a range of children's drink.

Retired in 1983 he was called back in the business to become Chairman of Hall and Woodhouse, following the deaths of his brewery cousins John and Edward.

John Woodhouse maintained a keen interest in history and forestry. In his younger days he was a keen skier and glider pilot. He married Peggy and enjoyed family life until her death in 1997. John was the only son of Brigadier Charles Woodhouse ex-Colonel of the Dorset Regiment.

Lieutenant Colonel John Woodhouse MBE MC, SAS passed away in 2008 aged eighty-five. He leaves two sons, Michael and William. Acknowledged by many as the founder of todays SAS, he will always to me, be the young Lieutenant whose kindness, bravery and attitude towards junior fellow soldiers made him an officer to be respected and admired and always to be remembered.

APPENDIX IV
ERIC GORDON MONSEY

I first met Eric when he appeared in front of the O.C. Battle Patrol and volunteered to join it following the tour of the companies by Lt. Woodhouse, a few days after Dennis and myself volunteered. We hit it off straight away and I found he was a Norfolk boy of about the same age as us. A quiet, friendly and unassuming lad, we trained and did many patrols together. I forget how long he had been in the Surreys but I believe he had also been in battles in North Africa and Sicily.

When the Battle Patrol disbanded we were posted to different companies and offered promotion and Lance Corporal Monsey continued in combat as the Battalion battled towards the north of Italy. At the Agenta Gap Eric was killed in action. It was the 23rd of April 1945. Eric was 20 years old. It has always been a sadness to me since I became aware of the date of his death, for seven days later Hitler committed suicide and the war was virtually over.

Eric is buried in the Agenta Gap War Cemetery in Italy and his name is also on the war memorial and in the parish church at Cawston, Norfolk.

APPENDIX V
REFLECTIONS

I'm sitting on a rock. The rock is on a hill. The day is bright. Shadows move across my body, beams of sunlight follow. I feel the warmth on the back of my hands, making kidney spots itch. There is no sound. I see fields below me. Verdant, softly green. Across the fields the distance fades into darker colours. Shells, mortars, bombs, sparking streams of red tracer descend gracefully into emptiness. Mud, earth and metal explode skywards in black, grey and scarlet unison. Toy figures darkly clothed rise silently from the earth and back towards me move forward steadily. Some sink back to the earth. Smaller and smaller become the figures. Then they are gone. There is no sound. I rise and enter the silent house.

Memories. I'm alone.

APPENDIX VI
MALAYSIAN MEDAL

In 2014 a small package came through my letter box. Inside was a neat blue box on which in gold was embossed the Arms of Malaysia and the inscription PINGAT JASA MALAYSIA.

I had been awarded the Malaysian Medal and on a polished silver coloured plaque was scripted the following:

PINGAT JASA MALAYSIA

"This medal is awarded to the peacekeeping groups amongst the communion countries for distinguished chivalry, gallantry, sacrifice or loyalty in upholding the Peninsula of Malaya or Malaysia sovereignty during the period of Emergency and Confrontation"

This good looking medal was for service in the fifties and sixties of the last century during the Emergency confrontation with the Communist Terrorists.

To receive a medal from fifty years after the event and when you have passed your ninetieth birthday on the planet is to have a pleasant surprise.

Printed in Great Britain
by Amazon